BASIC CANTONESE
A GRAMMAR AND WORKBOOK

Basic Cantonese introduces the essentials of Cantonese grammar in a straightforward and systematic way. Each of the 28 units deals with a grammatical topic and provides associated exercises, designed to put grammar into a communicative context. Special attention is paid to topics which differ from English and European language structures.

Features include:

- clear, accessible format
- lively examples to illustrate each grammar point
- informative keys to all exercises
- glossary of grammatical terms

Basic Cantonese is ideal for students new to the language. Together with its sister volume, *Intermediate Cantonese*, it forms a structured course of the essentials of Cantonese grammar.

Virginia Yip is Associate Professor at the Department of Modern Languages and Intercultural Studies, Chinese University of Hong Kong. **Stephen Matthews** lectures in the Department of Linguistics at the University of Hong Kong. They are the authors of *Cantonese: A Comprehensive Grammar (1994)*.

BASIC CANTONESE: A GRAMMAR AND WORKBOOK

Virginia Yip and Stephen Matthews

London and New York

First published 2000 by Routledge
11 New Fetter Lane, London EC4P 4EE

Simultaneously published in the USA and Canada
by Routledge
29 West 35th street, New York, NY 10001

Routledge is an imprint of the Taylor & Francis Group

Transferred to Digital Printing 2003

© 2000 Virginia Yip and Stephen Matthews

Typeset in Times by The Florence Group, Stoodleigh, Devon.

British Library Cataloguing in Publication Data
A catalogue record for this book is available from the British Library

Library of Congress Cataloging in Publication Data
Yip, Virginia, 1962–
    Basic cantonese : a grammar and workbook / Virginia Yip and Stephen
Matthews.
        p.   cm. – (Routledge grammars)
    Includes index.
    1. Cantonese dialects–Grammar. I. Matthews, Stephen, 1963–
II. Title. III. Series.
    PL1733.Y56   1999
    495.1'7–dc21   99–22788
                    CIP

ISBN 0–415–19384–2 (hbk)
ISBN 0–415–19385–0 (pbk)

For Timothy and Sophie,
fountains of creativity and inspiration

CONTENTS

INTRODUCTION

This book is for learners of Cantonese who aim to take their knowledge of the language beyond the phrase-book level. While our *Cantonese: A Comprehensive Grammar* was designed as a reference book, *Basic Cantonese* is more pedagogical in orientation. It highlights the key building blocks of sentence structure, leaving details of grammar and usage for the more advanced learner. It also provides practice for the grammar points of each unit in the form of communicatively oriented exercises.

The book is self-contained in the sense that it can be used on its own for self-paced learning. With the grammar points presented in approximate order of difficulty, it should also be useful for practice, revision and reference. It can be used in conjunction with a language course or lessons from a tutor. Either way, it should be understood that to learn a tone language such as Cantonese effectively requires some aural support – ideally from native speakers, or as a second best option from audiovisual materials such as tapes or CD-ROMs.

The Cantonese language

Cantonese is named after the city of Canton (known as Guangzhou in Mandarin), the capital of Guangdong province in southern China. Apart from the provinces of Guangdong and Guangxi, it is spoken in neighbouring Hong Kong and Macau, and also in Chinese communities overseas where it is often the predominant form of Chinese. Both in southern China and in Singapore and Malaysia, where it is widely spoken, it enjoys considerable prestige due to its association with the prosperous southern provinces as well as with the Cantonese culture of films and popular music ('Canto-pop'). It is also widely heard in cities such as Toronto and Vancouver in Canada, Sydney in Australia, New York and San Francisco in the USA. Cantonese will continue to be spoken widely around the Pacific Rim in the twenty-first century.

Cantonese is generally regarded, even by its own speakers, as a dialect of Chinese. This tends to imply, misleadingly, that it differs from standard Chinese (Mandarin or *Putonghua* 'common speech') largely in pronunciation, with some differences in vocabulary and relatively few in grammar. The grammatical differences are often underestimated, and it is dangerous to assume that the same Chinese grammar (essentially that of Mandarin) can be applied straightforwardly to Cantonese. In fact Cantonese has its own fully-fledged grammatical system, largely independent of Mandarin grammar. Indeed the Chinese 'dialects' vary in grammar, as they do in other respects, as much as the various Romance languages such as French, Spanish and Italian. Moreover, the dialects of southern China, which include Cantonese and Taiwanese, are especially distinctive and diverse. Naturally, some knowledge of Mandarin can be helpful in learning Cantonese, but one cannot assume that it is simply a matter of learning a new pronunciation for the same language, or a new set of vocabulary to go with the same grammar. Hence to learn Cantonese effectively one needs to pay attention to its grammar.

Cantonese grammar

Readers should be aware that the concept of 'grammar' used here is essentially that of contemporary linguistics, which is descriptive in approach, rather than that of traditional school grammar with its prescriptive concern for what is 'good' or 'correct'. The descriptive approach aims to capture the patterns of language as they are actually used by native speakers, without imposing value judgements on particular grammatical forms. Speakers of Cantonese are often puzzled by the idea of Cantonese, as a 'dialect', having its own grammar. Perhaps the simplest way to demonstrate that it does is to consider examples of 'Cantonese' as spoken by foreign learners, such as the following:

*Ngóh fāan ūkkéi chìh dī	I'll go home later
*Kéuih móuh heui-jó	He didn't go

These two sentences are unacceptable to a native speaker (the asterisk * marks them as ungrammatical), the first because in Cantonese adverbs of time such as chìh dī meaning 'later' come before the verb, not after as in English, and the second because the suffix -jó indicating completion is incompatible with most types of negative sentence. These explanations, simply put, are rules of grammar (the precise details are, of course, more complicated). By grammar, then, we mean the rules or principles governing the structure of sentences.

The kind of grammar to be learnt in mastering Cantonese, however, is not like that of Latin or Spanish where the forms of words – noun declensions, verb conjugations and the like – call for study. Instead, the more important questions are those of syntax: the order and patterns in which words are put together to form sentences. Sometimes Cantonese syntax resembles English:

leng sāam	pretty clothes
taai loih	too long
gwa héi	hang up
ngóh sīk kéuih	I know him

In other cases, the order of words is markedly different. In some of these features, Cantonese differs from English as well as from Mandarin – the construction with **béi** 'to give' being a well-known example:

Ngóh béi chín léih
(*lit.* I give money you)
I give you money

Where the syntax is likely to cause difficulty in following the examples, as in this case, we give a literal word-by-word gloss reflecting the Cantonese word order as well as the natural, idiomatic English translation. As a general principle we have aimed to do this where the English translation diverges substantially from the Cantonese original, as in the case of questions and 'topicalized' sentences:

Léih sihk mātyéh a?
(*lit.* you eat what)
What are you eating?

Tìhmbán ngóh m̀h sihk la
(*lit.* dessert I not eat)
I don't eat dessert

The glosses, within parentheses preceded by *lit.*, are generally omitted once a pattern has been established.

Chinese writing and romanization

The relationship of spoken Cantonese to Chinese writing is complicated. The Chinese writing system is based on Mandarin, the spoken language of Beijing and northern China. Although Cantonese can be written as it is spoken – with some difficulty, since many Cantonese words lack established characters – written Cantonese of this kind is hardly used for serious purposes, being largely confined to popular magazines and newspaper columns. For serious writing, standard Chinese is used instead. This standard written Chinese can then be read aloud with Cantonese 'readings' (pronunciations) for each character, which are taught in schools in Hong Kong and Macau, enabling educated Cantonese speakers to be literate in standard Chinese while speaking only Cantonese.

For most western learners wishing to learn to read or write Chinese, however, it will be useful to do so in conjunction with spoken Mandarin, rather than Cantonese alone. For these reasons, we have not included characters, but use the Yale romanization system (with the minor modifications introduced in our *Cantonese: A Comprehensive Grammar*). This system has proved effective for learners and is used in most language courses, textbooks, dictionaries and glossaries. The main disadvantage of the Yale system is that most native speakers are unfamiliar with it, and therefore find it quite difficult to read: it should be considered merely as an aid to learning the spoken language.

Pronunciation

Beyond grammar, one of the main difficulties of Cantonese is posed by its pronunciation, and tones in particular. For this reason, the first three chapters are devoted to establishing and reinforcing the main features of Cantonese pronunciation. Learners who do not have access to native speakers or Cantonese media should be sure to acquire some tapes or other audiovisual materials in order to practise recognition and production of tones.

Exercises

The exercises in this book are intended to be communicatively useful tasks, rather than the mechanical rote practice of some past grammars. The emphasis is placed on expressing ideas and, to give them a more authentic feel, some are situated in a real-life context: ordering dishes in a restaurant, asking for directions, and the like. Because many of the exercises are open-ended, they naturally allow more than one answer: the suggested answers given in the key by no means represent the only options. Learners with access to native speakers may benefit from reading out their own answers to them and eliciting alternatives. More demanding exercises, which may require additional knowledge or reference to other units, are marked with a dagger (†).

Further practice

Few learners will be satisfied with armchair knowledge of the language: to put grammatical knowledge to practical use, exposure to Cantonese media and practice with native speakers will be needed. This book aims to provide a firm foundation on which to build proficiency. Using the minimum of terminology, it should provide just enough grammatical apparatus for the teacher and learner to devise further practice activities of their own. Readers graduating from this book will also be able to progress to *Intermediate Cantonese* which takes them into new and more challenging territory.

UNIT ONE
Consonants

In Cantonese it is useful to distinguish initial consonants, that is those which occur at the beginning of a syllable, from those found at the end of a syllable.

Initial consonants

	Unaspirated	Aspirated	Fricative	Nasal/ liquid
Bilabial	b	p	f	m
Dental/alveolar	d	t	s	n/l
Velar/glottal	g	k	h	ng
Labio-velar	gw	kw		
Alveolar affricates	j	ch		

The consonant sounds in the third and fourth columns – the fricatives **f**, **s**, **h** and the nasals **m**, **n**, **ng** – are pronounced much as in English, while the first two columns pose greater difficulty. Whereas English stops such as **p** and **b** are distinguished by the fact that **p** is voiceless and **b** voiced, no Cantonese stops are distinctively voiced; instead they are distinguished by aspiration – a burst of air emitted in the process of articulation. In English, this feature is also present in that initial **p** is normally aspirated and **b** not; however, this contrast is not a distinctive one. To an English speaker, Cantonese **b** as in **béi** 'give' may sound either like **p** (because of the lack of voicing) or like **b** (because of the lack of aspiration). This combination of features – voiceless and unaspirated – is not found in English, making the Cantonese consonants **b/d/g** difficult to recognize and produce at first. Remember that **b-** as in **bāt** 'pen', **d-** as in **deui** 'pair' and **g-** as in **gwai** 'expensive' are not voiced. The problem also arises in romanized place names: *Kowloon*, for example, is generally pronounced by English speakers with an aspirated [k], but in the Cantonese form **Gáulùhng** the initial consonant is not aspirated.

In the labio-velar consonants **gw** and **kw**, the initial velar consonant is articulated more or less simultaneously with the bilabial [w] as in **gwa** 'hang' and **kwàhn** 'skirt'. There is a tendency to simplify **gw** and **kw** to [g] and [k] respectively before **o** or **u**, e.g. **gwok** 'country' sounds identical to **gok** 'feel'. Similarly:

Gwóngjāu	→	**Góngjāu** Canton (Guangzhou)
gwú	→	**gú** guess
gwun	→	**gun** can (of beer, Coke, etc.)
kwòhng	→	**kòhng** crazy

The affricates **j** and **ch** are probably the most difficult of the initial consonants. They are distinguished by aspiration: **ch** is accompanied by a breath of air while **j** is not. There are two rather different pronunciations for each consonant, depending on the following vowel:

(i) Before the front vowels **i**, **yu** and **eu** or **eui** they are alveo-palatal, [tʃ] and [tʃʻ] respectively, formed with the tongue touching both the alveolar ridge and the palate:

jī	know	**chī**	to stick
jyū	pig	**chyūn**	village
jēui	chase	**chēui**	to blow

In these cases the sounds are fairly close to their English counterparts as in 'June' and 'choose'.

(ii) In all other cases they are alveolar, [ts] and [tsʻ] respectively, formed at the front of the mouth (like **d** and **t**) at the alveolar ridge just behind the teeth:

jā	to drive	**chàh**	tea
johng	crash	**cho**	wrong

These sounds are different from any in English: **chàh** should not be pronounced like 'char'. In all cases remember that the Cantonese **j** is not voiced, just as **d** is not, while **ch** as in **chín** is aspirated, like **t**.

Consonants and names

The romanized forms of names used in Hong Kong and south China follow various older transcription systems which can be confusing for the learner. To pronounce them correctly, bear in mind the following correspondences:

Place name	Yale romanization	Surname	Yale romanization
Kowloon	Gáulùhng	Kong	Gōng
Kwun Tong	Gwūn Tòhng	Kwok	Gwok
Tai Po	Daaih Bou	Tang	Dahng
Tsimtsatsui	Jīmsājéui	Tse	Jeh
Shatin	Sātìhn	Shek	Sehk

Semivowels

The semivowels **w-** and **y-** also occur at the beginning of a syllable. They can be pronounced much as in English:

w-	**wah**	say	**wúih**	will
y-	**yiu**	want	**yuhng**	use

In the case of initial **y-** followed by the vowel **yu**, technically we would have **yyu**, but this is conventionally written more simply as **yu**, as in **yuht** 'month'.

Nasals

The velar nasal written as **ng-** is a single consonant which presents two problems:

- It is basically the same sound that we find in 'sing' and 'singer', but in Cantonese it can begin a syllable, as in **ngóh** 'I'. It can be produced by pronouncing 'singer' as 'si-nger'.
- Cantonese speakers frequently do not pronounce it where expected. Thus the pronoun 'I' is often heard as **óh**, 'duck' is either **ngaap** or **aap**, while **ńgh** 'five' may be pronounced as **ḿh** instead.

A similar problem arises with the distinction between **n** and **l** which is made in dictionaries and some textbooks. Although certain words nominally begin with **n**, notably the pronoun **néih** 'you', most speakers pronounce these with **l** instead:

néuih-yán	or	**léuih-yán** woman
nám	or	**lám** think
nīdouh	or	**līdouh** here

Syllabic nasals

The nasal consonants **m** and **ng** occur as syllables in their own right, albeit only in a few words. The most frequently encountered examples are:

m̀h	not (the main negative word: see Unit 14)
ńgh	five (also pronounced **m̀h**: see above)
Ǹgh	Ng (a common surname)

Note that these words each carry a tone of their own.

Final consonants

Only two kinds of consonants occur at the end of a syllable:

- the stops **-p**, **-t**, **-k**: these stops are unreleased, i.e. the airstream is closed to make them, but not reopened again, so that no air is released. Such consonants occur in casual pronunciation in English (e.g. 'yep!') as well as in German and many other languages, and are not difficult to produce. What is more difficult is to hear the difference between them, as they tend to sound alike:

  baat (eight) vs. **(yāt) baak** ((one) hundred)
  sāp chē (wet car) vs. **sāt chē** (missing car) vs. **sāk chē** (traffic jam)

- the nasals **-m**, **-n**, **-ng**: these are easily pronounced, although Mandarin speakers may have difficulty with **-m**.

  sāam (three) vs. **sāan** (to close) vs. **sāang** (alive)
  làahm (south) vs. **làahn** (difficult) vs. **láahng** (cold)

One complication here is that many speakers pronounce the **-ng** words with **-n** in certain syllables, so that **hohksāang** 'student', for example, is pronounced **hohksāan**.

Exercise 1.1

Pronounce the following words paying special attention to the consonants. You may need to look at Unit 2 (vowels) and Unit 3 (tone) in order to pronounce the words correctly. If possible check your pronunciation with a native speaker.

1 **baat** eight
2 **taap** tower
3 **je** lend/borrow
4 **ngoh** hungry
5 **ngāam** exactly
6 **luhk** six
7 **seun** letter
8 **cheung** sing
9 **ńgh** five
10 **yaht** day

Exercise 1.2

The following words are 'minimal pairs' differing in only one feature. Identify this difference and make sure that your pronunciation distinguishes the two words.

1 **bin** change   **pin** a slice
2 **baai** worship   **paai** distribute
3 **daai** bring   **taai** too (excessively)
4 **dīn** mad   **tīn** sky
5 **jēui** chase   **chēui** blow
6 **jēun** bottle   **chēun** spring
7 **gok** feel   **kok** accurate
8 **gau** enough   **kau** deduct
9 **gwan** stick   **kwan** difficult
10 **jēung** sheet (of paper) **chēung** window

† Exercise 1.3

The following surnames (1–6) and place names (7–12) are written in obsolete romanization systems. Pronounce them and write them in Yale romanization.

1 **Cheung**   7 **Tai O**
2 **Chiu**   8 **Lai Chi Kok**

3 **Kwan**
4 **Ting**
5 **Shum**
6 **Chung**

9 **Tseung Kwan O**
10 **Shaukeiwan**
11 **Tai Kok Tsui**
12 **Sham Shui Po**

UNIT TWO
Vowels and diphthongs

The vowels written **a**, **aa**, **e**, **i**, **o**, **u**, **eu** and **yu** are all single vowels which should be pronounced with consistent quality throughout: for example, Cantonese **so** should not sound like 'so' in English, but more like 'saw'. The first six are comparable to English vowels, while the last two are not, being closer to French:

a	**bāt** pen	similar to the vowel in 'but'
aa	**sāam** three	similar to the vowel in 'father'
i	**sī** silk	similar to the vowel in 'see'
e	**leng** pretty	similar to the vowel in 'pet'
o	**dō** many	similar to the vowel in 'paw'
u	**fu** trousers	similar to the vowel in 'fool'
yu	**syū** book	similar to the vowel in French 'tu'
eu	**seun** letter	similar to the first vowel in French 'Peugeot'

Long and short a

A peculiarity of Cantonese not shared with most other varieties of Chinese is the distinction between short **a** and long **aa**. The following minimal pairs differ in the length of the vowel:

sām	heart	**sāam**	three
mahn	ask	**maahn**	slow
hàhng	permanent	**hàahng**	walk
kāt	cough	**kāat**	card

These vowels differ in sound quality as well as length: **sām** sounds much like English 'sum', while **sāam** has an open vowel more like that of 'sample' in (southern British) English. When **a** comes at the end of a syllable as in **fa** 'flower' it is written with a single **a** but pronounced as in 'fa-ther'.

Front rounded vowels

The digraphs **yu** and **eu** represent single vowels produced at the front of the mouth with rounded lips; counterparts to these are not generally used in English, but exist in several European languages:

yu is similar to French 'u' and German 'ü'. In English something like it appears in the second syllable of 'issue'.

eu is similar to French 'eu' as in the second syllable in 'hors d'oeuvre'. English speakers may try pronouncing 'her' with rounded lips (as if pouting).

Variable vowels

The sound of a vowel can be affected by a following consonant. In particular, high vowels become more open before the velar consonants **-k** and **-ng**:

1 The vowel in **sihk** 'eat' lies between **i** and **e**, but is still distinct from **sehk** 'stone'. Similarly, **gīng** 'pass by' can be difficult to distinguish from **gēng** 'be afraid'. In a few words usage varies between **i** and **e**, for example, **sìhng** or **sèhng** 'whole'.
2 The vowel in **luhk** 'green' lies between **u** and **o**, but is still distinct from **lohk** 'go down'. Similarly, **tùhng** 'with' can be difficult to distinguish from **tòhng** 'sugar'.
3 The rounded vowel **eu** before the velar consonants **k** and **ng** as in **jeuk** 'wear' and **cheung** 'sing' is more open than that in **chēut** 'go out', **jēun** 'bottle', **seun** 'letter', and so on.

Diphthongs

These combinations of two vowel sounds are produced by shifting from one vowel to another over the course of one syllable:

iu	**giu**	call(ed)	as in English 'few'
oi	**choi**	vegetable	as in English 'boy'
ou	**dou**	arrive	as in English 'hold'
ei	**sei**	four	as in English 'say'
ui	**guih**	tired	as in English 'goo-ey '(but pronounced as only one syllable)
eui	**seui**	tax	(the front rounded vowel **eu** followed by the glide **i**)

Note that there are diphthongs corresponding to both short **a** and long **aa**:

ai	sāi	west	aai	sāai	to waste
	máih	rice		máaih	to buy
au	gau	enough	aau	gaau	to teach
	lauh	leak		laauh	to scold

The long diphthongs are close to those in English: **aai** is similar to that in 'sky', **aau** to that in 'how'.

Exercise 2.1

Pronounce the following minimal pairs (refer to Unit 3 for the tones, which are the same for each pair):

1	gān	follow	gāan	(classifier for house)
2	fān	separate	fāan	back, return
3	sān	new	sāan	mountain
4	gām	gold	gāam	prison
5	lám	think	láam	hug, embrace
6	gám	dare	gáam	deduct, reduce (prices)
7	làhm	to water	làahm	blue
8	gāi	chicken	gāai	street
9	láih	polite	láaih	milk
10	chāu	autumn	chāau	copy
11	ling	shiny	leng	pretty
12	pìhng	flat	pèhng	cheap
13	līk	take, pick	lēk	clever, smart
14	sihk	eat	sehk	stone
15	gīng	pass	gēng	fear
16	mohk	curtain, screen	muhk	wood
17	song	lose, die	sung	send
18	lohk	happy	luhk	green
19	dohk	measure	duhk	read
20	mohng	to stare	muhng	dream

Exercise 2.2

Pronounce the following words, paying special attention to the rounded vowels **yu** and **eu** (if possible check your pronunciation with a native speaker or against a recording):

1	**syut**	snow	11	**yuhbeih**	prepare
2	**hyut**	blood	12	**kyutdihng**	decide
3	**hēung**	fragrant	13	**yuhtbéng**	mooncake
4	**kèuhng**	strong	14	**leuhnjeuhn**	clumsy
5	**yuhnyi**	willing	15	**màauhtéuhn**	contradiction
6	**chyun**	to spell/an inch			
7	**lyuhn**	chaotic, messy			
8	**jēun**	bottle			
9	**jyuh**	to live			
10	**dyún**	short			

Exercise 2.3

Pronounce the following pairs of words paying special attention to the diphthongs:

A monosyllabic			B disyllabic	
1	**meih**	not yet	**meihdouh**	taste
2	**gei**	mail	**jihgéi**	oneself
3	**yiu**	want	**jiugu**	take care
4	**siu**	smile	**diu-yú**	fishing
5	**tiu**	jump	**tiu-móuh**	to dance
6	**múih**	every, each	**mùihmúi**	sister
7	**míuh**	seconds	**kèihmiuh**	wonderful
8	**guih**	tired	**hauhfui**	regret
9	**giu**	call	**gīu-ngouh**	proud
10	**wúih**	will	**hōi-wúi**	have a meeting
11	**dói**	bag	**joigin**	see you (*lit.* see again)
12	**gói**	change	**yīnggōi**	should
13	**gōu**	tall	**gwónggou**	advertisement
14	**lóuh**	old	**dihnlóuh**	computer
15	**tēui**	push	**teui-yāu**	retire

UNIT THREE
Tone

Like other varieties of Chinese and many south-east Asian languages, Cantonese is a tonal language: the relative pitch at which a syllable is pronounced plays a role in distinguishing one word from another. While tone presents one of the biggest obstacles, both real and psychological, to a working command of Cantonese, it also gives a musical quality to the language, and some learners find musical analogies helpful.

The importance of tones

Whereas in other languages deviation in pitch might merely result in a foreign accent, in Cantonese it changes the identity of a word:

High level		Low level		Mid level		Low level	
sān	new	**sahn**	kidney	**gau**	enough	**gauh**	old, dated
syū	book	**syuh**	tree	**dim**	to touch	**dihm**	OK, done

High level		High rising		High rising		Low rising	
lāu	jacket	**láu**	apartment	**ngó**	goose	**ngóh**	I
yāt bun	one half	**yāt bún**	one (book)	**chí**	teeth	**chíh**	resemble

Fortunately a word pronounced with an inaccurate tone can often be recognized from the context, although the errors are sometimes amusing.

How many tones?

To begin with a perennial question: how many tones are there? Linguists of different persuasions debate the issue, and different dialects of Cantonese vary in this respect. Although some reference books distinguish seven, nine or even ten tones, most current analyses assume six in

Hong Kong Cantonese – and for the beginner six tones are plenty. These are shown, with the vowel **a** as an example, in the following table.

	Rising	Level	Falling
High		ā	
	á		(à)
Mid		a	
	áh		
Low		ah	àh

The 'high level' tone is sometimes pronounced with a noticeable fall (à) as in **sìn** 'first'. Some books and dictionaries attempt to distinguish high level as in **sāan** 'hill' from high falling as in **sàan** 'to close', but most speakers make no such systematic distinction and these two words sound identical. Some other textbooks show this tone as 'falling' (à) for typographical convenience; we write them with the 'high level' diacritic (ā) throughout as this pronunciation seems to be dominant among younger speakers in Hong Kong.

For many beginners, two strategies may be useful in tackling the six tones:

- The three level tones (high, mid and low) are relatively easy to recognize and produce, providing three anchor points. In musical terms, the difference between the high and mid-level tones is about one and a half tones (a minor third), while that between the mid-level and low-level tones is one whole tone.
- It is relatively easy to recognize a tone as being one of the higher or one of the lower three. The 'h' marking the three low tones in the Yale romanization system comes in useful here, effectively marking the lower register. To distinguish between the various lower tones, especially between the low level and low falling, is more demanding. The low falling tone as in **làih** 'come' can often be recognized by a 'creaky' voice quality as the pitch reaches the bottom of the speaker's voice range.

The pronunciations are best learnt from native speakers or recordings, but English intonation patterns approximate some of the tones:

- The high rising tone as in **dím** 'how?' resembles a question showing surprise ('who? really??');
- The low rising tone as in **ngóh** 'I' begins with a slight dip and can be compared to a hesitant 'well, . . .';
- The low falling tone as in **yàhn** 'person' resembles a dismissive intonation. as in a calm but definitive 'no'.

It may be some consolation to note that speakers of other Chinese dialects, and even some native speakers, have difficulty distinguishing the two rising tones, sometimes confusing phrases such as:

sung séung heui	send some pictures (**séung**)
sung séuhng heui	send something up (**séuhng**)
Méihgwok sí	American history
Méihgwok síh	the American market

Tone versus stress and intonation

In English a word such as 'yes' can be pronounced with a variety of intonation patterns:

- falling: yes! (We've done it!)
- dipping: yes, (but . . .)
- low level: yes . . . (What is it this time?)

In Cantonese the word **haih** 'yes' must be pronounced with a low-level tone regardless of the context, otherwise it will sound like another word. Word stress and intonation patterns as used in English and other European languages often interfere with production of tones. When we stress a word, we automatically give it a high pitch; if this is superimposed on a Cantonese tone, it may turn a low tone into a high level or high falling one, for example:

haih (yes) + emphatic stress → **hāi** or **hài** (this is a common error, often committed by the second author, and comes dangerously close to obscenity)

Similarly, questions in English and many other languages end with a rising intonation. If this is added to a Cantonese question it may change the identity of the last word or two. Consequently, the scope for stress and intonation is limited (largely to sentence particles).

Tone change

A 'changed tone' occurs in colloquial speech in certain combinations. The affected syllable is pronounced with a high rising tone instead of the usual low (level or falling) tone. There are several categories including the following:

(i) Nouns at the end of a compound or phrase:

yàhn person	but	**léuih-yán** woman
yuht month	but	**chóh-yút** spend a month recovering after giving birth
màhn-hohk literature	but	**Yīng-mán** English (language)
yùh-dáan fish-cake	but	**tìuh yú** a/the fish
làuh-tāi staircase	but	**déng-láu** top floor, penthouse
yāt *hahp* **syū** a box of books	but	**yāt go** *háp* a box
yāt *dihp* **choi** a dish of vegetables	but	**yāt jek** *díp* a dish

(ii) Names with the prefix **a-** or **lóuh-**:

Chàhn Sāang Mr. Chan	but	**A-Chán** Chan (colloquial)
Làih Sāang Mr Lai		**Lóuh-Lái** old (Mr) Lai

(iii) Reduplicated adjectives, in which the second syllable changes to a high rising tone (see also Unit 9):

sòh foolish	but	**sòh-só-déi** silly
fèih fat	but	**fèih-féi-déi** chubby

The rules underlying this alternation are rather too complex to spell out here. Learners will develop a feel for this phenomenon on exposure to colloquial Cantonese.

Exercise 3.1

Practise distinguishing the six tones on the following syllables (meanings given in parentheses indicate that the syllable forms part of a word with that meaning):

1	**sī**	**sí**	**si**	**sìh**	**síh**	**sih**
	poem	history	try	time	market	matter
2	**fān**	**fán**	**fan**	**fàhn**	**fáhn**	**fahn**
	split	powder	lie	grave	(excited)	portion
3	**sēui**	**séui**	**seui**	**sèuih**	**séuih**	**seuih**
	need	water	tax	suspend	(clue)	(tunnel)
4	**yāu**	**yáu**	**yau**	**yàuh**	**yáuh**	**yauh**
	rest	petrol	slender	swim	have	again
5	**fū**	**fú**	**fu**	**fùh**	**fúh**	**fuh**
	(husband)	bitter	trousers	support	woman	father

Exercise 3.2

Read out the following sentences which illustrate the same sequence of six tones as in exercise 3.1:

1 **Dī gú-piu kòhng séuhng lohk** (The shares are going up and down (in value) like crazy)
2 **Ūkkéi gam kùhng móuh yuhng** (The household is so poor, it's no use)
3 **Gām lín gwai m̀h máaih jyuh** (This year it's expensive, (we) won't buy it yet)
4 **Sān láu taai làahn máaih maaih** (New flats are too difficult to buy and sell)
5 **Bīn gwái go tùhng kéuih jyuh?** (Who on earth is living with him?)
6 **Jīng hóu saai sèhng máahn sihk** (After steaming everything, spend the whole evening eating it)

Exercise 3.3

Pronounce the following pairs differing in tone (and occasionally other features such as vowel length):

1 **fóchē**	train	**fochē**	lorry
2 **chīsin**	crazy	**chìhsihn**	charity
3 **lóuh yàhn**	old person	**louh yàhn**	pedestrian
4 **gāaisíh**	market	**gai sìh**	count the time
5 **sái sān**	to wash one's body	**sái sahn**	clean the kidney (dialysis)
6 **lāangsāam**	sweater	**laahn sāam**	worn-out clothes
7 **gúsíh**	stock market	**gusih**	story
8 **maaih láu**	sell a flat	**máaih láu**	buy a jacket
9 **gáu dím**	9 o'clock	**gáau dihm**	manage to do something
10 **sēung mòhng**	casualty	**séuhng móhng**	get on the Internet

† Exercise 3.4

Change the tone of the italicized syllable or word to the high-rising changed tone as used in colloquial speech, for example, **sān** new + *màhn* information → **sānmán** news:

1 **hauh** behind + *mùhn* door → _____   back door
2 **yàuh** oil + *tiuh* strip → _____   Chinese fried doughnut
3 **bun** half + *yeh* late → _____   midnight

4   **sīu** burn + *yeh* late → _____   late-night meal
5   **Dāk** German + *màhn* language → _____   German
6   **tīn** sky + *pàahng* scaffolding → _____   roof top
7   **sāam jek** three-classifier + *dihp* dish → _____   three dishes
8   **Ou** bay + *mùhn* door → _____   Macau (place name)
9   **yahp** put in + *yàuh* oil → _____   fill up with petrol
10   **fā** flower + *yùhn* garden → _____   garden

UNIT FOUR
Pronouns

The personal pronouns make a good place to begin an initiation into Cantonese grammar, since they are rather straightforward: they do not vary according to gender, case or social status. Nor are there any possessive forms as such, since the pronouns combine with the possessive **ge** to indicate possession (see Unit 5). The plural forms are produced in regular fashion by adding the suffix **-deih** to the corresponding singular forms.

Person	Singular	Plural
first: I, we	ngóh (óh)	ngóhdeih (óhdeih)
second: you	néih (léih)	néihdeih (léihdeih)
third: he/she, they	kéuih (héuih)	kéuihdeih (héuihdeih)

Notice that each of the pronoun forms has alternative pronunciations. The forms in brackets are the result of sound changes, and are the object of a certain amount of controversy: courses rarely teach them; teachers may treat them as incorrect, and television advertising campaigns have even sought to outlaw them. Nevertheless in the case of 'you' **léih** has become by far the most common form, with initial **l-** replacing **n-**, while **óh** and **héuih** are also commonly heard.

The suffix -deih

One of the few grammatical suffixes in the language, the suffix **-deih** cannot be used to form plural forms of nouns (e.g. we cannot use ***sīnsāang-deih** to mean 'teachers'). Apart from the personal pronouns as shown above, its only uses are:

(i)   In the form **yàhn-deih** which serves as a kind of indefinite pronoun (people, one, etc.):

Yàhndeih tái-jyuh léih   People are watching you
Mhóu chou yàhndeih   Don't disturb (other) people

This form can also be used to refer indirectly to oneself:

A: **Léih dímgáai m̀h chēut sēng ga?**   Why don't you say anything?
B: **Yàhndeih mhóuyisi a**   Maybe I'm embarrassed

(ii)   In contracted forms with names, as in:

Paul kéuihdeih → Paul-deih   Paul and his family/friends
A-Chán kéuihdeih → A-Chán-deih   Chan and his family/company, etc.

Using pronouns

Pronouns are used to refer to individuals, as in introductions:

Ngóh giu Stephen   My name is Stephen
Ngóh haih go hohksāang   I'm a student
Kéuih haih Méihgwokyàhn   He's American
Ngóhdeih haih yàuhhaak   We're tourists

As in many languages (such as Italian, Spanish and Japanese) pronouns can be omitted when they are understood from the context. Some typical examples of such contexts follow:

A: **Heui bīndouh a?**
     (*lit.* go where?)
     Where are you going?

B: **Fāan ūkkéi**
     (*lit.* return home)
     I'm going home

A: **A-Yīng jouh mātyéh gūng ga?**
     (*lit.* Ying does what job?)
     What does Ying do for a living?

B: **Jouh wuhsih ge**
(*lit.* does nurse)
She's a nurse

Note that this also applies to objects, as in the following cases:

A: **Yám-m̀h-yám jáu a?**
(*lit.* drink wine or not?)
Would you like some wine?

B: **M̀h yám la, mgōi saai**
(*lit.* not drink, thanks a lot)
I won't, thanks

A: **Nī go sung béi léih ge**
(*lit.* this give to you)
This is for you

B: **Dōjeh! Ngóh hóu jūngyi a!**
(*lit.* thank you! I very much like!)
Thank you! I like it!

Again, when several statements are made about the same subject, it is usually understood after its first mention. If you are introducing yourself, for example, it is sufficient to use **ngóh** once:

Ngóh giu Mary, gām lín sahp-baat seui, làih Hēunggóng jouh gāauwuhn hohksāang
(*lit.* I called Mary, this year eighteen years old, come Hong Kong as exchange student)
My name is Mary, [I'm] eighteen this year, [I] came to Hong Kong as an exchange student

The third person: he, she and it

The third-person pronoun **kéuih** means 'he' or 'she', without distinction of gender. It is not normally used to refer to inanimate things, and hence there is typically nothing corresponding to the English pronoun **it**, whether as subject or object of the verb. For example, referring to a picture or piece of clothing:

Hóu leng a! Ngóh yiu a!
(*lit.* very nice! I want)
It's beautiful! I want it!

Again, a sequence of statements can be made about the same topic:

Kéuih máaih-jó ga sān chē hóu gwai ge, hóu chói kéuih taaitáai dōu jūngyi jēk
(*lit.* he bought a new car, very expensive, fortunately his wife also likes)
He's bought a new car, [it was] very expensive, fortunately his wife likes [it] too

Similarly, there is no counterpart to 'it' referring to the weather, or to nothing in particular:

Gāmyaht hóu yiht a
(*lit.* today very hot)
It's hot today

Lohk yúh la!
(*lit.* falls rain)
It's raining!

Hóu làahn góng
(*lit.* very hard to say)
It's hard to say

Reflexive jihgéi

The reflexive form **jihgéi** is used for all persons: myself, yourself, herself, ourselves, etc. It is used:

(i) Alone, referring back to the subject of the sentence:

Léih yiu síusām jiugu jihgéi
(*lit.* you should carefully look after yourself)
You should look after yourself carefully

Mhóu sèhngyaht gwaai jihgéi
(*lit.* don't always blame yourself)
Don't blame yourself all the time

Kéuih deui jihgéi hóu yáuh-seunsām
(*lit.* he towards himself very confident)
He has confidence in himself

(ii) Reinforcing a pronoun:

Ngóh jihgéi m̀h wúih gám jouh
(*lit.* I myself not would so behave)
I myself would not behave like that

Léih jihgéi sīn jī daap-on
(*lit.* you self only know answer)
Only you yourself know the answer

A-Yān sèhngyaht jaan *kéuih jihgéi*
(*lit.* Yan always praise her self)
Yan is always praising herself

(iii) As an adverb meaning 'by oneself':

Ngóh jihgéi máaih sung jyú faahn
(*lit.* I myself buy groceries cook rice)
I'll buy the groceries and cook by myself

Léih yīnggōi jihgéi lám chīngchó
(*lit.* you should yourself think clearly)
You should think things over by yourself

Kéuih séung jihgéi jouh haih-jyúyahm
(*lit.* he want self do department chairperson)
He wants to be the department chairperson himself

Exercise 4.1

Supply the missing pronouns:

1	_____ jyuh hái Gáulùhng	*I* live in Kowloon
2	**Hóu hōisām gin dóu** _____	Glad to see *you*
3	_____ sīk _____	*We* know *them*
4	_____ haih go hóu yīsāng	*You* are a nice doctor
5	_____ haih hohksāang	*You* are students
6	_____ hóu jūngyi yāmngohk	*He* likes music
7	_____ dá-jó-dihnwá béi lóuhbáan	*I* phoned the boss
8	_____ heui-gwo Oumún	*They*'ve been to Macau
9	_____ geidāk _____	*She* remembered *me*
10	_____ hóu gwa-jyuh _____	*They* missed *us* very much

Exercise 4.2

Replace the italicized phrases with pronouns in the following sentences:

1 *Síu Mìhng* hóu lengjái — Ming is very handsome
2 Ngóh heui taam *ngóh a-màh* — I'm going to visit my grandmother
3 Máh yīsāng yī-hóu-jó *géi go behngyàhn* — Dr Ma has cured several patients
4 Susan ga-jó *John* go sailóu — Susan has married John's brother
5 *Dī hohksāang* ge gūngfo taai dō la — The students' homework is too much
6 *Lóuhbáan tùhng go beisyū* git-jó-fān — The boss and the secretary got married
7 Ngóh hóu gwa-jyuh *go léui* — I'm missing my daughter very much
8 Kéuih tái-jó *dī tùhngsih* ge seun — She read her colleagues' letter(s)
9 *Ngóh tùhng ngóh sailóu* yātchàih hahpjok — My brother and I collaborate together
10 *Léih tùhng go jái* hóu chíhyéung — You and your son look like each other

† Exercise 4.3

Answer the following questions, considering whether a pronoun is needed or not:

1 Léih jūng-m̀h-jūngyi Hēunggóng a? — Do you like Hong Kong?
2 Kàhmyaht tīnhei dím a? — How was the weather yesterday?
3 Bīngo hóyíh bōng ngóh a? — Who can help me?
4 Léih tóuh-m̀h-tóuh-ngoh a? — Are you hungry?
5 Kéuihdeih jáu-jó meih a? — Have they left?
6 Kéuih je-jó chín béi bīngo a? — Who did he lend money to?
7 Léih maaih-jó ga chē meih a? — Have you sold the car?
8 Fūk wá leng-m̀h-leng a? — Is the picture beautiful?
9 Ga chē jíng hóu meih a? — Is the car mended?
10 Dī gúpiu yáuh-móuh sīng a? — Have the shares gone up?

UNIT FIVE
Possession: ge

ge is one of the most frequent words in Cantonese, used in several important grammatical patterns. One of its main uses is to indicate possession, as we can illustrate with the pronouns introduced in Unit 4:

ngóh ge	my, mine	**ngóhdeih ge**	our, ours
léih ge	your, yours	**léihdeih ge**	your, yours
kéuih ge	his/her, hers	**kéuihdeih ge**	their, theirs
jihgéi ge	one's own	**bīngo ge**	whose

As the two translations suggest, these are used in two ways:

1 Before a possessed noun:

Ngóh ge deihjí hái nīdouh	My address is here
Léih ge Gwóngdūng-wá m̀h cho	Your Cantonese is not bad
Kéuih ge gihnhōng mhaih géi hóu	Her health is not too good
Jihgéi ge gātìhng jeui gányiu	One's own family is most important

2 As predicates, usually following the verb **haih** 'be' (see Unit 7):

Nī go haih léih ge	This is yours
Dī chín haih kéuih ge	The money is his
Haih-mhaih ngóh ge?	Is it mine?

The verb **haih** 'be' can also be understood, so that the resulting sentence lacks a verb:

Bá jē kéuih ge	This umbrella is hers
Jek māau kéuihdeih ge	The cat is theirs
Nī tìuh sósìh bīngo ge?	Whose key is this?

Some points to notice:

- The **ge** indicating possession is sometimes omitted, especially where there is a close intrinsic relationship between the possessor and possessed, as in the case of relatives and family members:

kéuih sailóu	her younger brother
ngóh lóuhgūng	my husband (colloquial)
léih gūjē	your aunt (father's younger sister)

These phrases can themselves serve as the possessor of another noun:

Kéuih sailóu ge mahntàih hóu dō
Her (younger) brother's problems are many

Ngóh lóuhgūng ge ūkkéi-yàhn làih saai
My husband's family have all come

Léih gūjē ge mahtyihp hóu jihk-chín
Your aunt's property is worth a lot money

- Before nouns, the appropriate classifier (see Unit 8) is often used in place of **ge**, especially in colloquial language:

ngóh go léui	my daughter
kéuih ga chē	his car
léih gihn sāam	your shirt

This has a similar meaning to the corresponding phrase with **ge**, but denotes a particular individual or object. To specify more than one, the plural classifier **dī** is used:

ngóh dī jáiléui	my children
kéuih dī sāam	her clothes
Peter dī hohksāang	Peter's students

See Unit 8 for more on classifiers.

Exercise 5.1

Express the following by using the possessive marker provided (i.e. classifier, **ge** or **dī**):

Example: my book (**syū: bún**) → **ngóh bún syū**

1 your nose (**beih: go**)
2 her friends (**pàhngyáuh: ge/dī**)
3 her eyes (**ngáahn: deui**)
4 his desk (**tói: jēung**)
5 my letters (**seun: ge/dī**)
6 her handbag (**sáudói: go**)
7 my foot (**geuk: jek**)
8 Hong Kong's weather (**tīnhei: ge**)
9 today's news (**sānmán: ge/dī**)
10 tomorrow's temperature (**heiwān: ge**)

Exercise 5.2

Express the following by using the appropriate possessive marker:

Example: Your computer is too slow → **Ngóh go dihnlóuh taai maahn**

1 Compliment someone on their shoes (**deui hàaih**)
   _____ _____ hàaih hóu leng wo
2 Ask for the price of your friend's coat (**gihn lāu**)
   _____ _____ lāu géi dō chín a?
3 Describe Hong Kong's airport (**go gēichèuhng**) to a friend
   _____ _____ gēichèuhng hóu daaih ga
4 Your sports car (**ga páauchē**) has broken down
   _____ _____ páauchē waaih-jó
5 More than one of your relatives (**chānchīk**) is coming to see you
   _____ _____ chānchīk làih taam ngóh
6 Your wife (**taaitáai**) is waiting for you
   _____ taaitáai dáng-gán ngóh
7 Your son (**jái**) likes to sing
   _____ _____ jái jūngyi cheung-gō
8 Your children (**jáiléui**) are in secondary school
   _____ _____ jáiléui duhk-gán jūnghohk

Exercise 5.3

Translate into Cantonese:

1 This watch (**jek sáubīu**) is mine
2 The piano (**go gongkàhm**) is hers
3 That house (**gāan ūk**) is theirs

4 These books (**dī syū**) are yours
5 Those pictures (**dī wá**) are Miss Chan's
6 This place (**go wái**) is ours
7 This office (**go baahn-gūng-sāt**) is Mr Lam's
8 The money (**dī chín**) is my wife's

UNIT SIX
Possession and existence: yáuh

The verb **yáuh**, like 'have' in English, serves both as a main verb ('I have a question') and as an auxiliary ('Have you sent the letter?'). Like all verbs in Cantonese, it keeps the same form for different persons:

Ngóh yáuh yāt go jái yāt go léui   I have a son and a daughter
Léih juhng yáuh gēiwuih   You still have a chance
Kéuih yáuh géi gāan ūk   She has several houses

Unusually, however, it has one irregular form: **móuh** is the negative form of **yáuh**. So, 'I don't have' is **ngóh móuh** (not *ngóh m̀h yáuh):

Léih móuh gīngyihm   You don't have experience
Ngóhdeih móuh sailouhjái   We don't have any children
Kéuihdeih móuh ūkkéi   They don't have a home

The question form is composed by putting **yáuh** 'have' and **móuh** 'not have' together as **yáuh-móuh** (not *yáuh-m̀h-yáuh):

Léih yáuh-móuh mahntàih a?   Do you have any questions?
Ngóhdeih yáuh-móuh sìhgaan a? Do we have time?
Kéuihdeih yáuh-móuh chín a?   Do they have money?

See Unit 23 for more on questions of this kind.

Existential yáuh

yáuh can also mean 'there is' (like Spanish 'hay', French 'il y a', etc.). Similarly, **móuh** can mean 'There is not' and **yáuh-móuh** 'Is there …?':

Hēunggóng yáuh hóu dō dīksí
(*lit.* Hong Kong have very many taxis)
There are lots of taxis in Hong Kong

Nīdouh móuh hùhngmāau
(*lit.* here not-have pandas)
There are no pandas here

Tói seuhngmihn yáuh géi jek díp
(*lit.* table on-top have a few plates)
There are a few plates on the table

Notice that no preposition is needed: the sentence simply begins with the place expression (see Unit 13).
   yáuh in this sense also serves to introduce an indefinite noun phrase:

Yáuh (yāt) go yàhn wán léih   (not *Yāt go yàhn wán léih)
(*lit.* have a person seeking you)
A man is looking for you

Yáuh géi go hohksāang hóu lāu
(*lit.* have several students very angry)
Several students are angry

Yáuh hóu dō haakyàhn làih-jó
(*lit.* have many guests came)
Many guests came

A verb can be added to show what is to be done with the item introduced by **yáuh/móuh**:

Ngóh gāmyaht yáuh gūngfo jouh
(*lit.* I today have homework to do)
I have homework to do today

Nīdouh móuh sāam máaih
(*lit.* here have no clothes to buy)
There are no clothes to buy here

Yahpbihn yáuh-móuh yéh sihk a?
(*lit.* inside have or have not anything to eat)
Is there anything to eat inside?

Note that there is no need to distinguish infinitives from the regular form of the verb.

yáuh as auxiliary

yáuh also serves as an auxiliary verb, rather like 'have' in English 'They have left', but normally only in the negative form móuh and in questions as yáuh-móuh:

Kéuih gāmyaht móuh fāan-gūng   He hasn't been to work today
Ngóh móuh jouh-gwo sīnsāang   I've never been a teacher

A: Kéuihdeih yáuh-móuh būn ūk a?   Have they moved house?
B: Yáuh a (būn-jó la)   Yes (they have)
A: Léih yáuh-móuh hohk-gwo   Have you learnt Putonghua?
   Póutūng-wá a?
B: Móuh a (móuh hohk-gwo a)   No (I haven't)

Note the close relationship here between yáuh/móuh and the aspect markers jó and gwo (gwo can appear in sentences with móuh or yáuh-móuh but jó cannot: see Unit 18). The use of yáuh alone as an auxiliary is rare, but a useful idiom is yáuh lohk 'Someone's getting off' (used on minibuses, and so on to express the wish to get off):

Yáuh lohk, mgōi   (Someone's) getting off, please
Chìhnmihn yáuh lohk   (Someone's) getting off just ahead

Adjectives formed with yáuh

yáuh and móuh can also be added to nouns to form adjectives:

yáuh	+	chín money	→	yáuh-chín	rich
yáuh	+	sām heart	→	yáuh-sām	thoughtful, kind
yáuh	+	yuhng use	→	yáuh-yuhng	useful
móuh	+	yuhng use	→	móuh-yuhng	useless
yáuh	+	líu substance	→	yáuh-líu	substantial, learned
móuh	+	líu substance	→	móuh-líu	vacuous, ignorant

The adjectives thus formed can then be modified in the usual way (see Unit 9):

Dōjeh léihdeih gam yáuh-sām
Thank you for being so thoughtful

Kéuih lóuhgūng hóu yáuh-chín, bātgwo taai móuh-líu
Her husband is very rich but too vacuous

Exercise 6.1

Turn the following statements into questions, positive or negative statements as specified:

Example: **Ngóh yáuh mahntàih** I have a problem → negative: **Ngóh
móuh mahntàih**

1 **Ngóh yáuh yigin** (I have an opinion) → negative
2 **Léih yáuh beimaht** (You have a secret) → question
3 **Gāmyaht yáuh sīusīk** (Today we have the latest information) →
   negative
4 **Faatgwok yáuh Jūnggwokyàhn** (There are Chinese people in France)
   → question
5 **Chēutbihn móuh yàhn** (There's nobody outside) → positive
6 **Kéuih yáuh behng** (She has a disease) → negative
7 **Léih yáuh láihmaht** (You have a gift) → question
8 **Bún syū yáuh Jūngmàhnjih** (There are Chinese characters in the book)
   → negative
9 **Sātìhn yáuh fóchē-jaahm** (There's a railway station at Shatin) → question
10 **Kàhmyaht móuh taaiyèuhng** (There was no sunshine yesterday) →
   positive

Exercise 6.2

Answer the following questions about yourself using **yáuh** or **móuh** as
appropriate:

1 **Léih yáuh-móuh yāt baak mān a** ($100)?
2 **Léih hái Hēunggóng yáuh-móuh pàhngyáuh a** (friends)?
3 **Léihdeih yáuh-móuh dihnlóuh a** (computer)?
4 **Léih gāan fóng yáuh-móuh hūngwái a** (space in your room)?
5 **Léih yáuh-móuh sìhgaan hohk Gwóngdūng-wá a** (time to study
   Cantonese)?
6 **Léihdeih yáuh-móuh heui-gwo Gwóngjāu a** (been to Guangzhou)?
7 **Léih gāmyaht yáuh-móuh tái sānmán a** (watch the news today)?

8 **Léih yáuh-móuh hingcheui jyun gūng a** (interested in changing your job)?

Exercise 6.3

Translate these questions into Cantonese:

1 Do you have a car (**chē**)?
2 Do you have brothers or sisters (**hīngdaih jímuih**)?
3 Do you have a mobile phone (**sáutàih dihnwá**)?
4 Have you been to Beijing (**Bākgīng**)?
5 Has she visited (**taam-gwo**) you?
6 There are no birds (**jeukjái**) here.
7 There are many minibuses (**síubā**) in Hong Kong.
8 Is there anybody inside (**yahpbihn**)?
9 Are there students in the classroom (**fosāt**)?
10 Is there any good news (**hóu sīusīk**) today?

UNIT SEVEN
Being: haih

The verb **haih** 'to be' is straightforward in form, but used in ways which do not always match those of English and other European languages. It is used to introduce noun phrases, as in making introductions and identifying people:

Ngóh haih Chàhn Síu Mìhng	I'm Chan Siu Ming
Léih haih bīngo a?	Who are you?
Kéuih haih yīsāng	She's a doctor

As we saw in Unit 5, many such statements can also be made without **haih**, especially when a sentence particle such as the explanatory **lèihga** is added (see Unit 25):

	Nī go haih ngóh làahm-pàhngyáuh	This is my boyfriend
or	**Nī go ngóh làahm-pàhngyáuh (lèihga)**	
	Ngóhdeih haih Chìuhjāuyàhn	We are Chiu Chow (people)
or	**Ngóhdeih Chìuhjāuyàhn (lèihga)**	

Note in particular that **haih** is not used with predicative adjectives, which are typically introduced by **hóu** (*lit.* 'very': see Unit 9):

Ngóh yìhgā hóu mòhng	I'm busy now
(not ***Ngóh yìhgā haih hóu mòhng**)	
Léih gājē hóu leng	Your (elder) sister is beautiful
(not ***Léih gājē haih hóu leng**)	
Ngóh tùhng kéuih hóu suhk	I know him well (*lit.* I with
	him familiar)
(not ***Ngóh tùhng kéuih haih hóu suhk**)	

haih **showing agreement**

haih also serves to indicate agreement and as an answer to certain types
of question, **haih** meaning 'yes' and its negative form **mhaih** 'no':

A: **Hóu gwai wo**   It's very expensive
B: **Haih a**   Yes, it is

A: **Léih jānhaih seun mē?**   Do you really believe it?
B: **Mhaih a**   No, I don't

haih should not be taken simply as a counterpart to 'yes', however, since:

(i) **haih** can indicate agreement with a negative sentence:

A: **Léih m̀h seun àh?**   Don't you believe it?
B: **Haih a**   No (I don't)

A: **Kéuihdeih meih dou mē?**   Haven't they arrived yet?
B: **Haih a**   No (they haven't)

(ii) The most common types of question do not take **haih** for an answer.
     Instead, the verb of the original question is repeated (see Unit 23):

A: **Ngóhdeih heui-m̀h-heui**   Are we going shopping?
   máaih yéh a?
B: **Heui a**   Yes (not *haih)

A: **Léih jūng-m̀h-jūngyi a?** Do you like it?
B: **Jūngyi a**   Yes (not *haih)

haih **versus** hái

Notice the difference in tone between **haih** and **hái**, which can also be
translated as 'be' but in the sense of being located:

haih	be	e.g.	**Kéuih haih Yahtbúnyàhn**	She's Japanese
			Kéuih haih haauhjéung	He's the principal
hái	be at/in	e.g.	**Kéuih hái Seuhnghói**	She's in Shanghai
			Ngóh hái syūfóng	I'm in the study

Emphatic haih and ge

haih can serve to emphasize the following word(s), especially in concert with the particle ge at the end of the sentence:

> **Haih léih bōng ngóh ge**   (emphasizing the subject **léih**)
> It was you who helped me

> **Nī bún syū haih bīngo sung ga?** (emphasizing the subject **bīngo**)
> (*lit.* this book is who gave)
> Who was it that gave (us) this book?

> **Fūng seun haih gāmyaht gei dou ge** (emphasizing the adverb **gāmyaht**)
> (*lit.* the letter is today arrived)
> It was today the letter arrived

This formula is especially useful because, Cantonese being a tone language, there is limited scope for emphasizing a word through stress as is commonly done in English as in 'The letter arrived *today*'. The particle **ge** is characteristic of assertions (see Unit 25).

Exercise 7.1

Answer the questions affirmatively or negatively as indicated. Add the particle **a** for politeness.

1	**Léih chìh dou àh?**	Are you late? (answer: no)
2	**Léih héi-jó-sān làh?**	Have you woken up? (yes)
3	**Léih behng-jó àh?**	Are you sick? (no)
4	**Kéuih jáu-jó mē?**	Has he left? (yes)
5	**Léih gin-gwo ngóh mē?**	Have you seen me before? (no)
6	**Kéuih sīk léih ge mē?**	Does she know you? (no)
7	**Kéuih fan-jó làh?**	Has she fallen asleep? (yes)
8	**Kéuih yāusīk-gán àh?**	Is he resting? (yes)
9	**Kéuih hóu guih àh?**	Is he tired? (yes)
10	**Máh gaausauh hōi-gán wúi àh?**	Is Professor Ma having a meeting? (no)
11	**Léih m̀h sīk kéuih mē?**	Don't you know him? (no)
12	**Léih msái fāan gūng àh?**	Don't you need to go to work? (no)

Exercise 7.2

Choose **haih** or **hái** as required:

1	**Kéuihdeih _____ Méihgwokyàhn**	They are American
2	**Kéuih _____ ngóh sailóu**	He's my brother
3	**Kéuih _____ hohkhaauh**	She's at school
4	**Kéuihdeih m̀h _____ Hēunggóng**	They are not in Hong Kong
5	**Ngóh _____ Seuhnghóiyàhn**	I'm Shanghainese
6	**Go dói _____ kéuih ge**	The bag is his
7	**Léih Sāang _____ gūngsī**	Mr Lee is at the office
8	**Ngóhdeih _____ pàhngyáuh**	We're friends
9	**Ngóh go jái _____ ūkkéi**	My son is home
10	**Kéuih _____ ngóh tùhnghohk**	He's my classmate

† Exercise 7.3

Use **haih** and **ge** to emphasize the italicized word(s):

Example: **Ngóh *gaau* Yīngmán** I teach English → **Ngóh haih gaau Yīngmán ge**

1	***Lóuhbáan* góng béi ngóh tēng**	*The boss* told me
2	***Ngóh* béi bún syū léih**	*I* gave you the book
3	**Kéuih *gām jīu* jáu**	He left *this morning*
4	**Gihn sāam *géisìh* máaih**	*When* was this shirt bought?
5	**Go chēung *bīngo* hōi?**	*Who* opened the window?
6	**Ngóh *hái nīdouh* dáng léih**	I'll wait for you *here*
7	***Kéuih taaitáai* wán dóu**	*His wife* found it
8	**Kéuih *hái Taaigwok* johng chē**	He had a car crash *in Thailand*

UNIT EIGHT
Noun classifiers

To refer to a certain number of items, Cantonese (like other varieties of Chinese and many Asian languages) calls for a classifier (or measure) after the number. While in English relatively few nouns have such words associated with them, (for example 'a brace of pheasants', 'twenty head of cattle'), in Cantonese all nouns have such words and they must be used, for example:

yāt *go* yàhn	one person
léuhng *tìuh* yú	two fish
sei *jek* gáu	four dogs
sahp *tou* hei	ten films

Classifiers pose two different problems:

(i) which one to use with which noun;
(ii) when and where to use them.

First, however, it is useful to distinguish some sub-types of classifier.

Measures

These are in the narrow sense words used in counting quantities as in 'two dozen eggs':

léuhng *bohng* ngàuhyuhk	two pounds of beef
yāt *gān* choi	a catty of vegetables (1 catty = 22 ounces)
bun *dā* gāidáan	half a dozen eggs

Containers

These form an open-ended category since any container can serve as a measure:

sāam būi chàh	three cups of tea
léuhng hahp tóng	two boxes of sweets
yāt bāau máih	a bag of (uncooked) rice
yāt dihp choi	a dish of vegetables

These container words can also be used as nouns in their own right, in which case they generally take the classifier **go**:

yāt go wún	a bowl	léuhng go háp	two boxes
dō yāt go būi	another glass/cup	géi jek díp	several plates

Collective classifiers

These refer to a grouping of items:

nī bāan hohksāang	this class of students
gó dēui laahpsaap	that pile of rubbish
yāt daahp syū	a pile of books
yāt tou sān sāam	a set of new clothes
gó deui hàaih	that pair of shoes

Unfortunately, not all things that are treated as pairs in English take **deui**: 'a pair of trousers' is **yāt tìuh fu**, 'a pair of scissors' **yāt bá gaaujín**. On the other hand, there are other uses of **deui** which are understandable:

ngóh deui sáu
(*lit.* my pair (of) hands)
my (two) hands

yāt deui fūfúh
(*lit.* one pair couple)
a (married) couple

nī deui māléui
(*lit.* this pair twin girls)
these twin girls

Plurals and quantities with dī

The word **dī** can be seen as a special kind of measure, or more precisely as a collective classifier. It is used for both countable and uncountable nouns:

(a) referring to an unspecified number of countable items:

Dī cháang hóu tìhm	The oranges are nice and sweet
Ngóh heui taam dī pàhngyáuh	I'm going to visit some friends
Kéuih dī tùhngsih taai mòhng	Her colleagues are too busy

(b) referring to quantities of uncountable substances:

Dī séui m̀h gau yiht	The water is not hot enough
Ngóh yiu máaih dī sīnnáaih	I need to buy some fresh milk
Léih dī chàh hóu hēung	Your tea smells good

Which classifier?

There are dozens of different classifiers, from the ubiquitous **go** to very specific items like **bún** in **bún syū** 'the book'. As the term suggests, classifiers generally serve to sort nouns into semantic classes of objects:

Classifier	Semantic class	Examples	
bá	tools, instruments	**bá dōu**	knife
ga	machines, vehicles	**ga chē**	the car
gāan	buildings	**gāan ūk**	the house
gihn	most clothes	**gihn sāam**	shirt, dress
go	people	**yāt go yīsāng**	a doctor
	abstract things	**nī go kyutdihng**	this decision
		yāt go muhng	a dream
jek	most animals	**jek gáu**	a dog
	one of a pair	**yāt jek sáu**	one hand

A further important criterion is that many common classifiers categorize objects by their shape:

Classifier	Characteristics	Examples	
faai	vertical surface	**yāt faai geng**	a mirror
fūk	square/rectangular	**yāt fūk wá**	a picture
jēung	flat surface	**yāt jēung tói**	a table
jī	cylindrical	**jī bāt**	a pen/pencil

lāp	small and round	yāt lāp tóng	a sweet
tìuh	long and narrow	tìuh louh	the road

The shape criterion can override the semantic class criterion, so that animals and items of clothing distinguished by their elongated shape take tìuh, rather than **jek** or **gihn**:

tìuh yú	fish	tìuh kwàhn	skirt/dress
tìuh sèh	snake	tìuh fu	trousers

The appropriate classifier (or measure) can usually be checked in a dictionary, although it should be borne in mind that alternative classifiers may exist for the same noun. A computer, for example, is classified variously as a machine (**yāt bouh dihnlóuh**), or as a mere object (**yāt go dihnlóuh**).

Using classifiers

The main cases in which a classifier must be used are (illustrated with the commonest classifiers, such as **go**):

(i) Following a number:

yāt go yīsāng	one doctor	sāam go yàhn	three people
léuhng go dihnlóuh	two computers	sahp go háp	ten boxes

(ii) With the demonstratives **nī** or **lī** 'this' and **gó** 'that':

nī go sailouh	this child	gó go behngyàhn	that patient
nī go yínyùhn	this actor	gó go chēung	that window

While these usages may be familiar to readers who know Mandarin, two other important uses are more characteristically Cantonese:

(iii) In a possessive construction:

ngóh go jái	my son	kéuih gāan fóng	her room
léih gihn sāam	your dress	léihdeih chàhng láu	your flat

This is a colloquial alternative to the possessive construction with **ge** (see Unit 5).

(iv) With a noun alone:

go hohksāang	a/the student	**go gaausauh**	a/the professor
gihn sāam	a/the dress	**jek gáujái**	a/the puppy

This usage typically refers to a particular item. When the noun it goes with comes before the verb it is definite (generally corresponding to 'the'):

Gihn sāam hóu gwai	The dress is expensive
Ga chē jáu-jó	The car has gone
Go waih hóu tung	The stomach hurts

When the classifier and noun come after the verb it can be definite, but can also refer to an indefinite, but specific item ('a certain . . .'):

Kéuih máaih-jó gihn sāam	She's bought a/the dress
Ngóh gāmyaht tái-jó bún syū	I read a/the book today
Kéuihdeih hōi-jó go wuhháu	They opened an/the account

Exercise 8.1

Fill the gap with a suitable measure:

1 **yāt** _____ **baahkchoi** (Chinese cabbage)
2 **bun** _____ **mùihgwaifā** (roses)
3 **yāt** _____ **seun** (letter)
4 **yāt** _____ **jyūyuhk** (pork)
5 **yāt** _____ **sìhgaan** (time)
6 **léuhng** _____ **bējáu** (beer)
7 **yāt** _____ **tō-háai** (slippers)
8 **géi** _____ **sāijōng** (suit)

Exercise 8.2

Order the following items at a restaurant, adding **mgōi** for politeness at the beginning or end of the sentence (see Unit 27):

1 two glasses (**būi**) of red wine (**hùhng jáu**)
2 a dish (**dihp**) of fried noodles (**cháau mihn**)
3 three bowls (**wún**) of rice (**faahn**)
4 another pair (**deui**) of chopsticks (**faaijí**)
5 a bottle (**jēun**) of water (**séui**)
6 a menu (**chāan-páai**)
7 two wine glasses (**jáu-būi**)

8 a pot (**wùh**) of hot water (**yiht séui**)
9 a piece (**gihn**) of cake (**daahn-gōu**)
10 a cup (**būi**) of coffee (**gafē**)

Exercise 8.3

Match the following items with the appropriate classifier or measure:

A clothing

1 **tāai** tie	a **gihn**
2 **hàaih** (one) shoe	b **tìuh**
3 **sāijōng** suit	c **déng**
4 **móu** hat	d **jek**
5 **láu** coat	e **tou**

B stationery

1 **gaaujín** scissors	a **fūk**
2 **bāt** pen	b **bá**
3 **báan** board	c **jēung**
4 **yàuh-wá** oil painting	d **jī**
5 **kāatpín** business card	e **faai**

Exercise 8.4

Choose the appropriate classifier to replace **ge** in the following possessive expressions:

1 **kéuih ge sáubīu** her watch	a **jēung**
2 **lóuhbáan ge tói** the boss's desk	b **tìuh**
3 **gó chàhng láu ge mùhn** the door of that flat	c **jek**
4 **ngóh ge sósìh** my key	d **ga**
5 **léih ge séunggēi** your camera	e **douh**

UNIT NINE
Adjectives

Adjectives are words which denote properties or qualities. Typically they serve to modify or describe nouns, and can also appear in comparative forms (see Unit 12). Since the dividing line between adjectives and verbs is not always clear, the Chinese equivalents of adjectives are often termed stative verbs. While learners need not worry about whether there 'are' adjectives in Cantonese, it is useful to remember that the words in question generally behave like verbs: that is, what applies to verbs generally applies to adjectives too.

Attributive adjectives

These modify the noun. All such adjectives come before the noun they modify:

pèhng ge sāam	cheap clothes
gwāai ge sailouhjái	good, obedient children
cho ge kyutdihng	a wrong decision

The particle **ge**, which we have already seen in possessive constructions (Unit 5), serves here to link the adjective and noun. The adjective can be modified by **hóu** 'very', **jeui** 'most', etc.:

hóu kàhnlihk ge hohksāang	hard-working students
jeui lìhnhēng ge boksih	the youngest PhD
gam daaih ge yínghéung	such a big influence

Predicative adjectives

These are used to state that something has a certain property. The verb
haih 'to be' is not used (see Unit 7), but instead the adverb **hóu** is usually
included:

Ngóh hóu hōisām	I'm happy
Dī tōng hóu hàahm	The soup is salty
Kéuih gihn sāam hóu leng	Her dress is beautiful
Gāmyaht hóu sāp	It's humid today

hóu by itself can mean 'good' or 'very', but when used in this way it
does not really mean 'very' but is merely part of the syntax of predicative
adjectives.

Modifying adjectives

Other modifiers such as **géi** 'quite' and **gam** 'so' can appear in place of
hóu, for example:

Dī gēipiu *géi* pèhng	The air tickets are quite cheap
Léih go sáutàih dihnlóuh *gam* gwai	Your laptop computer is so expensive
Go daahn-gōu *taai* tìhm	The cake is too sweet
Ōnchyùhn *jeui* gányiu	Safety is most important
Tìuh síng *gau (saai)* chèuhng	The string is (more than) long enough

Reduplicated adjectives

Another strategy to modify the meaning of an adjective is reduplication
together with the suffix **-déi**:

dīn crazy → **dīn-dīn-déi**	rather crazy
fú bitter → **fú-fú-déi**	rather bitter
sau thin → **sau-sáu-déi**	rather thin
tìhm sweet → **tìhm-tím-déi**	rather sweet
lyúhn warm → **lyúhn-lyún-déi**	rather warm
muhn bored/boring → **muhn-mún-déi**	rather bored (or boring)

Note the change to a high rising tone on the repeated syllable (see Unit
3): this happens in all cases except where the original tone is high *level*

(as in **dīn-dīn-déi** 'rather crazy') or already high rising (as in **fú-fú-déi** 'rather bitter'). These forms are used to qualify the force of an adjective:

Dī Jūng-yeuhk fú-fú-déi	Chinese medicine is rather bitter
Tìuh gāai sāp-sāp-déi	The street is a bit wet
Tou hei muhn-mún-déi	The film was fairly boring
Ngóh gokdāk muhn-mún-déi	I feel rather bored

Note that these forms are not used together with **hóu** or other modifiers such as **géi** 'quite':

Nī go gaausauh dīn-dīn-déi ge	This professor is pretty crazy
(not * **Nī go gaausauh hóu dīn-dīn-déi ge**)	
Go wuhsih fèih-féi-déi	The nurse is rather chubby
(not * **Go wuhsih géi fèih-féi-déi**)	

Such reduplicated forms are also used as adverbs (Unit 10).

Exercise 9.1

Use appropriate predicative adjectives to describe the following:

Example: the film on an aeroplane: **Tou hei hóu chèuhng** The film was long

1 your girlfriend
2 your children or your friend's children
3 a teacher you like
4 a colleague at work
5 your good points (to your boss)
6 your favourite film star
7 a car you would like to own
8 the food at school or university
9 the weather in Hong Kong
10 a novel you have been reading

Exercise 9.2

Add an appropriate attributive adjective to modify the following:

Example: **Ngóh gòhgō hái yāt gāan *hóu yáuh-méng ge* gūngsī jouh-yéh**
My (elder) brother works for a famous company

1 **Kéuih ūkkéi yáuh go _____**   At home there is a . . . living room
   haak-tēng
2 **Deuimihn yáuh gāan _____**   Across the street there is a . . .
   chāantēng   restaurant
3 **Ngóh jeui gahn tái-gwo bún _____** I have recently read a . . . book
   syū
4 **Ngóh séung yiu jek _____ gáu-jái** I would like a . . . puppy
5 **Ngóh tái-gwo yāt tou _____ hei**   I have seen a . . . film
6 **Ngóhdeih yáuh dī _____ gūngfo**   We have some . . . homework
7 **Kéuih ūkkéi yáuh go _____**   There is a . . . problem at his home
   mahntàih
8 **Ngóh yíhchìhn yáuh go _____**   I used to have a . . . teacher
   lóuhsī

Exercise 9.3

Substitute a modifier (e.g. **géi, gam, taai, gau saai**) for **hóu**:

1   **Ngóhdeih hóu múhnyi**   We are satisfied
2   **Kéuih hóu lēk**   She's smart (capable)
3   **Kéuihdeih hóu guih**   They're tired
4   **Dī sailouhjái hóu dākyi**   The children are cute
5   **Tou hei hóu lohngmaahn**   The film is romantic
6   **Kéuih dī tàuhfaat hóu dyún**   Her hair is very short
7   **Dī gāsī hóu pèhng**   The furniture is cheap
8   **Go gaausauh hóu yáuh-méng**   The professor is famous
9   **Go hohksāang hóu láahn**   The student is lazy
10 **Dī séung hóu leng**   The photos are pretty

Exercise 9.4

Form reduplicated adjectives to express the meaning based on the adjective provided, remembering the change of tone:

   Example: The baby is chubby (**fèih**) Go bìhbī fèih-féi-déi

1 This dish (**dihp sung**) is a bit hot (**laaht**)
2 The soup (**dī tōng**) is rather sour (**syūn**)
3 Your clothes (**dī sāam**) are a bit wet (**sāp**)
4 The weather (**tīnhei**) is rather cold (**dung**)
5 Her face (**faai mihn**) is rather round (**yùhn**)
6 Her eyes (**deui ngáahn**) are a little red (**hùhng**)

7   His office (**go baahn-gūng-sāt**) is rather messy (**lyuhn**)
8   The button (**lāp láu**) is rather loose (**sūng**)
9   Your glasses (**fu ngáahn-géng**) are rather fuzzy (**mùhng**)
10 Your husband (**lóuhgūng**) is a bit drunk (**jeui**)

UNIT TEN
Adverbs of manner

Several types of adverb phrase can be used to modify a verb or verb phrase:

- with **dāk**
- with **gám**
- with reduplication.

These types of adverb phrase are generally based on adjectives (see Unit 9).

1 Adverb phrases with dāk

The most general form of adverbial phrase is formed with **dāk** and an adjective after the verb. The order is thus: verb – **dāk** – adjective. As usual the adjective is normally preceded by a modifier such as **hóu** or **géi**, and so on (see Unit 9):

Ga chē hàahng dāk hóu maahn
(*lit.* the car travel manner very slow)
The car moves very slowly

Dī haakyàhn sihk dāk géi hōisām
(*lit.* the guests eat manner quite happy)
The guests are eating quite happily

Go góngsī góng dāk taai faai
(*lit.* the lecturer speak manner too fast)
The lecturer talks too fast

When the verb is followed by an object, the verb is repeated so that **dāk** immediately follows the verb:

Ngóh cheung-gō cheung dāk hóu chā
(*lit.* I sing songs sing manner very bad)
I sing very badly

Kéuih waahk-wá waahk dāk géi leng
(*lit.* she paints pictures paints manner quite nice)
She draws quite nicely

Léih góng-yéh góng dāk taai daaih-sēng
(*lit.* you speak things speak manner too big voice)
You speak too loud

2 Adverb phrases with gám

An adjective together with **gám** 'thus' forms an adverbial phrase which comes before the verb:

Dī gwūnjung hóu daaih-sēng gám paak-sáu
(*lit.* the audience very big voice thus clap hands)
The audience applauded loudly

Go yàuh-haak hóu yáuh-láihmaauh gám mahn ngóh
(*lit.* the tourist very politely thus asked me)
The tourist asked me very politely

Go sīgēi hóu daaih-lihk gám sāan mùhn
(*lit.* the driver very big-force thus closed door)
The driver closed the door hard

Note here also the use of **gám** by itself or **gám yéuhng** to mean 'in this way':

Ngóh m̀h wúih gám góng
I wouldn't put it like that

Kéuih m̀h yīnggōi gám yéung sái chín
He shouldn't waste money in this way

3 Reduplicated adverbs

A limited number of adverbs of manner are formed by repeating an adjective and adding the suffix **-déi**:

| gwāai | obedient | → | gwāai-gwāai-déi | obediently |
| hēng | light | → | hēng-hēng-déi | lightly |

These are placed before the verb they modify:

Léih yiu gwāai-gwāai-déi jouh gūngfo
(*lit.* you need obediently do homework)
You have to obediently do your homework

Yáuh yàhn hēng-hēng-déi paak mùhn
(*lit.* have person lightly knock door)
Someone knocked lightly on the door

A few such forms are also used without **-déi**:

| maahn | slow | → | maahn-máan hàahng | to walk slowly |
| hōi-sām | happy | → | hōi-hōi-sām-sām jouh yéh | to work happily |

Note that:

(i)   The repeated adverb may take on a changed tone (with a low tone becoming a high rising one: see Units 3 and 9):

jihng   quiet   →   **jihng-jíng-déi**   quietly

(ii) In adjectives with two syllables, each syllable is repeated separately:

| gáan-dāan | simple | → | gáan-gáan-dāan-dāan | simply |
| hīng-sūng | relaxed | → | hīng-hīng-sūng-sūng | in a relaxed manner |

All these forms of adverb come before the verb they modify:

Léih jihng-jíng-déi yahp heui lā
Go in quietly

Kéuih tāu-tāu-déi jáu-jó
He left secretly

Kéuih gáan-gáan-dāan-dāan gám hingjūk sāangyaht
She celebrated her birthday in a simple way

Ngóhdeih hīng-hīng-sūng-sūng, gáan-gáan-dāan-dāan gám douh-ga
We spend our holiday in a laid-back, simple style

Reduplicated adverbs, especially those of more than one syllable, can combine with **gám** as described in (ii) above:

Kéuih sòh-só-déi gám siu
He smiles in a foolish way

Léih syū-syū-fuhk-fuhk gám fan háidouh lā
Lie down here comfortably

Kéuihdeih háidouh hīng-hīng-sūng-sūng gám tēng gō
They're relaxing listening to songs

Exercise 10.1

Add the adverbial phrase provided to the following sentences:

1 **Kéuihdeih hàahng fāan ūkkéi**
They walk home slowly (**màahn-máan**)
2 **Kéuih gaaisiuh jihgéi**
He introduces himself excitedly (**hóu hīngfáhn gám**)
3 **Kéuih mahn-jó yāt go mahntàih**
He asked a question boldly (**hóu daaih-dáam gám**)
4 **Kéuih só-jó douh mùhn**
She locked the door carefully (**hóu síusám gám**)
5 **Ngóh go jái waak-jó géi fūk wá**
My son drew several pictures quickly (**hóu faai gám**)
6 **Kéuih hohk-gán Gwóngdūng-wá**
He is studying Cantonese diligently (**hóu lóuhlihk gám**)
7 **Dī hohksāang tēng-gán yín-góng**
The students are listening to the lecture attentively (**hóu làuhsām gám**)
8 **Dī Hēunggóng hohksāang yèhng-jó béichoi**
The Hong Kong students won the competition comfortably (**hóu hīngsūng gám**)
9 **Yi-ngoih faatsāang-jó**
The accident happened suddenly (**hóu dahtyìhn gám**)
10 **Ngóh jūngyi hingjūk sāangyaht**
I like to celebrate birthdays happily (**hōi-hōi-sām-sām gám**)

Exercise 10.2

Use **dāk** to create adverbial phrases using the adjectives provided, repeating the verb where necessary (as in numbers 6–10):

Example: **Kéuih jáu *dāk* hóu faai**   He runs quickly
            Kéuih jā-chē *jā dāk* hóu msíusām   He drives carelessly

1 **Léih sé _____ hóu hóu**   You write well
2 **Ga fēigēi fēi _____ hóu dāi**   The plane flies low
3 **Ngóhdeih fan _____ hóu syūfuhk**   We sleep comfortably
4 **Kéuihdeih wáan _____ hóu hōisām**   They play happily
5 **Kéuih tiu _____ hóu yúhn**   She jumps a long way
6 **Kéuih yíng-séung _____ _____ hóu leng**   She takes pictures well
7 **Ngóh yàuh-séui _____ _____ hóu maahn**   I swim slowly
8 **Kéuih cheung-gō _____ _____ hóu sai-sēng** She sings softly
9 **Ngóh jyú-faahn _____ _____ hóu faai**   I cook quickly
10 **Ngóh tiu-móuh _____ _____ hóu chā**   I dance badly

Exercise 10.3

Fill in the gaps with a suitable manner adverbial with **-gám**:

1 **Ngóh** (I) _____ **sé nī fūng seun** (write this letter)
2 **Ngóhdeih** (We) _____ **tái boují** (read the newspaper)
3 **Kéuih** (He) _____ **fan hái chòhng seuhngmihn** (sleep on the bed)
4 **Kéuihdeih** (They) _____ **jáu-jó** (have left)
5 **Léih Síujé** (Miss Lee) _____ **daap ngóh go mahntàih** (answer my question)
6 **Lóuhbáan** (The boss) _____ **sāan-jó douh mùhn** (closed the door)
7 **Yihp gaausauh** (Professor Yip) _____ **góng syū** (give a lecture)
8 **Dī hohksāang** (The students) _____ **tēng syū** (listen to the lecture)
9 **Go bìhbī** (The baby) _____ **wáan-gán** (playing)
10 **Kéuih** (She) _____ **haam-gán** (crying)

UNIT ELEVEN
Adverbs of time, frequency and duration

While the adverbs introduced in the previous unit describe the manner of action, those included in this unit are concerned with the way events take place in time.

1 Adverbs of time

Given that verbs do not indicate tense in Cantonese, adverbs are especially important in specifying when events take place:

Kéuih *yìhgā* juhng hái yīyún
She's still in hospital (now)

Kéuih *gójahnsìh* juhng hái yīyún
She was still in hospital (then)

Ngóh *jīkhāak* heui Yīnggwok taam léih
I'm going to visit you in England (right away)

Ngóh *daih-yih-sìh* heui Yīnggwok taam léih
I'll visit you in England (in the future)

In English the tense of the verb indicates when things take place, and the adverb can easily be omitted, while in Cantonese only the adverb indicates the time. Common adverbs include:

Present:	**yìhgā**	now	**gāmyaht**	today
Recent past:	**tàuhsīn**	just now	**ngāam-ngāam**	just
Past:	**yíhchìhn**	before	**búnlòih**	originally
	seuhng chi	last time	**gójahnsìh**	then
	kàhmyaht	yesterday	**chìhnyaht**	the day before yesterday

Future:	jīkhāak	right away	daih yih sìh,	in future
			daih-sìh	
	hah chi	next time	dousìh	when the time comes
	tīngyaht	tomorrow	hauhyaht	the day after tomorrow

These adverbs may come:

(a) Before the verb:

| Ngóhdeih yìhgā chēut heui | We're going out now |
| Kéuih ngāam-ngāam jáu-jó | He just left |

(b) Before the subject:

| Búnlòih ngóh séung duhk yīfō | Originally I wanted to study medicine |
| Tàuhsīn kéuih mgeidāk daai sósìh | Just now he forgot his keys |

2 Adverbs of frequency and duration

Useful adverbs to describe the frequency of an action include:

sèhngyaht	always	yāt chi	once
dōsou	mostly	léuhng chi	twice
yáuh(-jahn)-sìh	sometimes	sāam chi	three times
yāt sìh-sìh/yāt sí-sìh	occasionally	géi chi	several times
pìhngsìh	normally	tūngsèuhng	usually

múih 'each' can be used to form adverbial phrases:

| múih go yuht | every month | múih go sīngkèih | every week |

Note that several common time expressions of one syllable do not take a classifier, and can form reduplicated adverbs:

múih chi or chi-chi	every time	(not *múih go chi)
múih yaht or yaht-yaht	every day	(not *múih go yaht)
múih lìhn or lìhn-lìhn	every year	(not *múih go lìhn)
múih jīu or jīu-jīu	every morning	(not *múih go jīu)
múih máahn or máahn-máahn	every evening	(not *múih go máahn)

All these adverbs generally come before the verb:

Kéuih múih jīu luhk dím héi sān ge
(*lit.* he each morning six o'clock gets up)
He gets up at six every morning

Kéuih yaht-yaht sái-tàuh
(*lit.* she daily washes hair)
She washes her hair every day

Note the order in phrases such as the following describing the frequency of actions:

yāt lìhn yāt chi	once a year (*lit.* one year one time)
múih go yuht yāt chi	once a month (*lit.* each month one time)

Such phrases are often split up with the more general term coming before the verb and the more specific frequency expression after:

Ngóhdeih yāt lìhn heui yāt chi douh-ga
(*lit.* we one year go one time spend holiday)
We go on holiday once a year

Ngóhdeih lìhn-lìhn fāan heui yāt chi
(*lit.* we each year return go one time)
We go back once a year

Adverbs of frequency may come after the verb and object:

Ngóh heui-gwo Daaihluhk yāt chi	I've been to mainland China once
Ngóh gin-gwo yīsāng sāam chi	I've seen the doctor three times

Adverbs of both frequency and duration can be used in the following ways:

(i) Between the verb and the object:

Ngóh heui-gwo *yāt chi* **Daaihluhk**	I've been to the mainland once
Kéuih jyú-gwo *géi chi* **faahn**	He's cooked dinner a few times
Ngóh gāmyaht sái-gwo *léuhng chi* **tàuh**	I've washed my hair twice today
Ngóh gin-gwo *sāam chi* **yīsāng**	I've seen the doctor three times
Kéuih duhk-jó *sāam lìhn* **Jūngmán**	He has studied Chinese for three years

Ngóh diu-jó *sèhng yaht* **yú**	I've been fishing for a whole day
Ngóh tái-jó *yāt go jūngtàuh* **syū**	I've read for an hour
Kéuih sihk-jó *yāt go yuht* **yeuk**	She has been on medication for a month

(ii) After the verb and object, with repetition of the transitive verb as seen in Unit 10:

Kéuih háau-síh háau-gwo géi chi	She's taken the exam several times
Kéuih jyú-faahn jyú-gwo géi chi	He's cooked dinner a few times
Ngóh duhk Jūngmán duhk-jó sāam lìhn	I've been studying Chinese for three years (or: I studied Chinese for three years)
Kéuih jyuh yīyún jyuh-jó yāt go yuht	She's been in hospital for a month (or: She stayed in hospital for a month)

As the translations suggest, this construction can refer either to a period of time leading up to the present, or to a completed period in the past (see Unit 18 on the aspect marker **-jó**).

Exercise 11.1

Add a suitable adverb to the following, paying attention to the position of the adverb:

1 **Ngóh hái Jīmsājéui**
  I was in Tsimshatsui (yesterday)
2 **Kéuih dou-jó gēichèuhng**
  She arrived at the airport (just now)
3 **Ngóh gin-gwo kéuih**
  I've met him (before)
4 **Kéuihdeih jung-jó tàuh-jéung**
  They won the first prize (last time)
5 **Ngóhdeih juhng sai**
  We were still small (then)
6 **Ngóh jouh wuhsih ge**
  I used to be a nurse (originally)
7 **Ngóhdeih wán léih**
  We'll contact you (next time)

8   **Kéuih hóu lāu**
    He got angry (immediately)
9   **Ngóh chéng léih sihk-faahn**
    I'll treat you to a meal (in future)
10 **Ngóhdeih hái Méihgwok jyuh-gwo**
    We used to live in America (before)

Exercise 11.2

Say how often you engage in the following activities (fictitiously where necessary):

1   play tennis (**dá móhngkàuh**)
2   go swimming (**heui yàuh-séui**)
3   watch television (**tái dihnsih**)
4   read the newspaper (**tái boují**)
5   wash your hair (**sái tàuh**)
6   have a haircut (**jín tàuhfaat**)
7   buy groceries (**máaih sung**)
8   go to a concert (**heui yām-ngohk-wúi**)
9   eat ice cream (**sihk syutgōu**)
10 visit relatives (**taam chānchīk**)

Exercise 11.3

State how long you do the following every day:

1   play video games (**dá gēi**)
2   practise Cantonese (**lihn Gwóngdūngwá**)
3   talk on the phone (**góng dihnwá**)
4   cooking (**jyú-faahn**)
5   listen to music (**tēng yām-ngohk**)
6   reading (**tái-syū**)
7   chat with friends (**kīng-gái**)
8   stay on the Internet (**séuhng móhng**)
9   take a shower (**chūng lèuhng**)
10 write in a diary (**sé yahtgei**)

Exercise 11.4

Add an adverb of duration in the space provided. Note that the following sentences involve reduplication of the verb.

1	**Kéuih hōi wúi hōi-jó** _____	She has been in a meeting
2	**Ngóhdeih sihk-faan sihk-jó** _____	We have been having a meal
3	**Kéuihdeih dá bō dá-jó** _____	They have been playing a ball game
4	**Ngóh sé seun sé-jó** _____	I have been writing letters
5	**Kéuih gói gyún gói-jó** _____	She has been marking papers
6	**Lohk yú lohk-jó** _____	It's been raining
7	**Kéuih cheung-gō cheung-jó** _____	He's been singing
8	**Dī hohksāang jouh gūngfo jouh-jó** _____	The students have been doing homework
9	**Kéuihdeih aai-gāau aai-jó** _____	They've been arguing
10	**Kéuih jā-chē jā-jó** _____	He's been driving

UNIT TWELVE
Comparison: **gwo** and **dī**

In this unit we look at ways of making simple comparisons. In colloquial Cantonese there are two basic kinds of comparison:

(i)　Where two things are explicitly being compared, **gwo** is used to mean 'more (adjective) than (noun)'. The word order is similar to the English (and quite unlike that in Mandarin):

Jenny sai gwo ngóh	Jenny is younger than me
Baat láu hóu gwo yih láu	The eighth floor is better than the second floor
Nī deui gwai gwo gó deui	This pair is more expensive than that one

Note that **gwo** is also a verb meaning 'cross' or 'pass', so it is natural that it comes to mean 'surpass' in comparisons.

(ii)　If the object of comparison is not expressed (i.e. there is no 'than . . .'), **dī** is used instead:

Jenny sai dī	Jenny is younger
Baat láu hóu dī	The eighth floor is better
Gó deui gwai dī	That pair is more expensive

dī literally means 'a little' but here serves largely to indicate a difference between the two items with respect to some property.

Modifying comparisons

Both kinds of comparison can be modified by adverbs of degree such as **hóu dō** 'much' and **síu-síu** 'a little', as follows:

(i)   In comparisons with **gwo**, the adverb of degree is simply added at
      the end of the construction:

Léih lēk gwo kéuih hóu dō	You're much smarter than him
Kéuih gōu gwo léih síu-síu	She's a little taller than you
Ngóh daaih gwo kéuih yāt lìhn	I'm a year older than her

(ii) In comparisons where **dī** would normally be used, a degree word such
      as **hóu dō** 'a lot' replaces **dī**:

Nī go leng dī	→ **Nī go leng hóu dō**	This one is much nicer
Nī go gwai dī	→ **Nī go gwai síu-síu**	This one is a little more expensive
Nī go chúhng dī	→ **Nī go chúhng géi púih**	This one is several times heavier

The reason for this is that **dī** literally means 'a bit', so that to combine it
with an adverb like **hóu dō** 'a lot' would be a contradiction in terms. This
shows that **dī** as in **leng dī** is not really equivalent to the suffix **-er** in
English 'prettier', tempting though the equivalence may be.

   juhng 'even' can be applied to both the **gwo** and **dī** constructions, but
comes *before* the adjective:

Gām chi juhng hóu gwo seuhng chi	This time is even better than last time
Gám yéung juhng hóu (dī)	This way is even better

(**dī** can be omitted here since the presence of **juhng** implies that a comparison is being made.)

Alternative forms of comparison

An alternative to the **gwo** form of comparison uses **béi** 'compare'. The
word order is quite different since **béi** and the object of comparison come
before the adjective:

Hahtīn béi dūngtīn chèuhng
(*lit.* summer compare winter long)
Summer is longer than winter

Hēunggóng ge jáudim béi Bākgīng dō
(*lit.* Hong Kong's hotels compare Beijing more)
There are more hotels in Hong Kong than Beijing

A modifying phrase comes after the adjective, as with **gwo**:

Kéuih béi ngóh sai yāt lìhn
(*lit.* she compare me young(er) one year)
She's a year younger than me

Ngóh béi ngóh lóuhpòh daaih sāam seui
(*lit.* I compare my wife big three years)
I'm three years older than my wife

Being basically a feature of Mandarin and written Chinese, the comparison with **béi** is more formal than the **gwo** construction. Learners who know some Mandarin will be able to use the **béi** construction readily in Cantonese, while other beginners would do best to stick with the colloquial **gwo**. The **béi** form does allow some comparisons which would not be possible with **gwo**, such as those expressing a change of state:

Kéuih béi gauh-lín sau-jó
(*lit.* she compare last year got thinner)
She's got thinner since last year

Léih béi seuhng chi jeunbouh-jó
(*lit.* you compared last time improved)
You've improved since last time

Yet another alternative is to omit **gwo** but add a phrase showing the degree of difference:

Kéuih gōu yàhndeih yāt go tàuh
(*lit.* he tall people one head)
He's a head taller than everyone else

Ngóhdeih faai kéuih yāt bouh
(*lit.* we fast him one step)
We're a step ahead of him

This construction is commonly found with dimensional adjectives such as **daaih** and **sai**, which are often used in this way to mean 'older' and 'younger' respectively:

Léih gòhgō daaih léih géi dō a?
(*lit.* your brother big you how much?)
How much older is your brother than you?

Kéuih sai ngóh yāt lìhn
(*lit.* she small me one year)
She's a year younger than me

Comparison of adverbs

This involves combining the syntax of adverbs (Unit 10) with that of comparison; it thus comes for free in the sense that nothing new has to be learnt. Comparisons using **gwo, dī** or **béi** are added to adverbial constructions with **dāk:**

Kéuih tái dāk faai gwo ngóh
(*lit.* he read manner quick than me)
He reads faster than I do

Léih sé dāk leng dī
(*lit.* you write manner nicer)
You write better

Kéuihdeih béi ngóhdeih jouh dāk hóu
(*lit.* they compare us do manner well)
They do it better then we do

The main difficulty arises where the verb has an object and both are repeated (Unit 10):

Kéuih tái Jūngmán tái dāk faai gwo ngóh
(*lit.* he reads Chinese reads manner quick than me)
He reads Chinese more quickly than I do

Léih sé jih sé dāk leng dī
(*lit.* you write characters write manner nicer)
You write characters better

Kéuihdeih jouh sāangyi béi ngóhdeih jouh dāk hóu
(*lit.* they do business compare us do manner well)
They do business better then we do

Superlatives

Superlatives are expressed straightforwardly by **jeui**, or as a colloquial alternative by **ji:**

jeui leng	most beautiful	**ji lēk**	the smartest
jeui fōngbihn	most convenient	**ji pèhng**	the cheapest
jeui hīngfáhn	most excited	**ji jeng**	the best, coolest (slang)

These forms are typically used as follows:

(i) Attributively, with **ge**:

jeui fōngbihn ge jouhfaat	the most convenient method
jeui gányiu ge sīusīk	the most important news
ji pèhng ge gēipiu	the cheapest air tickets

(ii) Predicatively, with **haih**:

Gám yéuhng jeui fōngbihn	This way is the most convenient
Nī júng ji dái máaih	This kind is the best value

The order is often reversed beginning with the superlative expression as the subject:

Jeui fōngbihn haih nī go deihdím
(*lit.* most convenient is this location)
This location is most convenient

Ji pèhng haih nī jek pàaihjí
(*lit.* most cheap is this brand)
This brand is the cheapest

A point to note here is that the range in which the comparison is to be made is specified *before* the superlative form:

Hēunggóng jeui chēutméng ge gōsáu
(*lit.* Hong Kong most famous singer)
The most famous singer in Hong Kong

Chyùhn gwok jeui daaih ge ngàhnhòhng
(*lit.* whole country most big bank)
The biggest bank in the whole country

Gam dō jáulàuh jeui hóu-sihk haih nī gāan
(*lit.* so many restaurants most good-to-eat is this one)
This is the best of all the restaurants to eat at

This ordering illustrates a general tendency in Cantonese to put the more general, inclusive term before the more specific one.

Exercise 12.1

Decide whether the following comparisons would use **gwo** or **dī**, and translate as much of the sentence as you can into Cantonese:

1 It's warmer today
2 She's happier now
3 My friend is older than me
4 She's much taller than before
5 It's slower this time
6 This restaurant is cheaper than that one
7 I like dancing more than singing
8 Your idea is better

Exercise 12.2

Make any meaningful comparison between the following:

1 Today (**gāmyaht**) and yesterday (**kàhmyaht**)
2 Girls (**léuihjái**) and boys (**làahmjái**)
3 Shirts (**sēutsāam**) and ties (**léngtāai**)
4 Toronto (**Dōlèuhndō**) and London (**Lèuhndēun**)
5 Chinese (**Jūngmán**) and English (**Yīngmán**)
6 Swimming (**yàuh-séui**) and jogging (**páau-bouh**)
7 Cantonese food (**Gwóngdūng choi**) and Chiu Chow food (**Chìuhjāu choi**)
8 Doing business (**jouh sāangyi**) and teaching (**gaau-syū**)

Exercise 12.3

Make the following comparisons more explicit using the adverb given in brackets:

1 **Gām-lín dung gwo gauh-lín**
   This year is (much) colder than last year
2 **Gāmyaht lyúhn dī**
   It's (much) warmer today

3 **Léih dī tàuhfaat yìhgā dyún dī**
   Your hair is (a little) shorter now
4 **Hēunggóng gwai gwo nīdouh**
   Hong Kong is (several times) more expensive than here
5 **Ngóh guih gwo kéuih**
   I'm (even) more tired than she is
6 **Sihk faahn pèhng gwo sihk mihn**
   Eating rice is (even) cheaper than eating noodles
7 **Gām chi hohkfai béi seuhng chi gwai**
   This time the tuition is (a hundred dollars) more expensive than last time
8 **Kéuih gōu gwo ngóh**
   She is (three inches) taller than me

† Exercise 12.4

A Express the following comparisons colloquially with **gwo**:

   Example: **Fóchē béi bāsí faai** → **Fóchē faai gwo bāsí**
   The train is faster than the bus

1 **Hói-yú béi yéuhng-yú gwai**
   Wild fish are more expensive than farmed fish
2 **Hēungpín béi hùhng chàh hēung**
   Jasmine tea is more fragrant than black tea
3 **Làahnfā béi gūkfā leng**
   Orchids are prettier than chrysanthemums
4 **Go léui béi go jái daaih léuhng seui**
   The daughter is two years older than the son
5 **Nī bāan hohksāang béi gó bāan kàhnlihk**
   This class is more hard-working than that one

B Express the following comparisons with **béi**:

1 **Gauh hàaih syūfuhk gwo sān hàaih**
   Old shoes are more comfortable than new ones
2 **Yìhgā heui Oujāu yùhngyih gwo yíhchìhn**
   Going to Australia now is easier than before
3 **Gūngsī gām-lín jaahn dāk dō gwo gauh-lín**
   The company has earned more this year than last year
4 **Nī bún síusyut hóu-tái gwo daih yāt bún**
   This novel is better than the first one
5 **Léih gām chi jouh dāk hóu gwo seuhng chi**
   This time you're doing better than last time

UNIT THIRTEEN
Prepositions: space and time

Three important classes of words are involved in the expression of location. We shall introduce these before showing how they are used in combination.

1 Prepositions

hái	at/in/on (also **héung**)	**yàuh**	(starting) from
heung	towards	**lèih**	(away) from
tùhng	with	**gīng**	(passing) via

Some of these items are also known as coverbs, since they have certain characteristics of verbs (see *Intermediate Cantonese*).

2 Demonstrative terms, based on nī 'this' and gó 'that'

nīdouh	here (also **nīsyu**)	**gódouh**	there (also **gósyu**)
nībihn	over here, this way	**góbihn**	over there, that way
nītàuh	around here (in this area)	**gótàuh**	around there (in that area)

3 Localizers or postpositions indicating spatial relationships

seuhngbihn	on top of	**hahbihn**	below
chìhnbihn	in front of	**hauhbihn**	behind
yahpbihn	inside	**chēutbihn**	outside
léuihmihn	inside, within	**ngoihbihn**	outside
deuimihn	opposite	**jākbīn**	beside
jūnggāan	in the middle of	**jīgāan**	between

Note how these characteristically end in **bihn** or **mihn** meaning 'side' (the two forms being interchangeable in most cases).

Location

Using the words introduced above, several characteristic patterns are used to indicate location in space:

(i)   **hái** followed by names of places:

Dī sailouhjái hái gódouh	The children are over there
Kéuihdeih lēi màaih hái nīsyu	They are hiding here
Ngóh gāmyaht sèhng yaht hái ūkkéi	I was at home all day today
Kéuih hái Méihgwok duhk-syū	She studies in America
Ngóhdeih hái hohkhaauh hōi-wúi	We're having a meeting at school
Kéuih yìhgā m̀h hái gūngsī	She is not at the office at the moment

Note that the word **háidouh** 'to be here' is generally used instead of **hái nīdouh** when presence or absence is at issue. For example, on the telephone:

Léih sāang m̀h háidouh   Mr Lee is not here
(not * **Léih sāang m̀h hái nīdouh**)

háidouh is also used to express action in progress (progressive aspect: Unit 19).

(ii)   **hái** together with a localizer:

Yīsāng hái seuhngbihn	The doctor is upstairs
Heiyún hái deuimihn	The cinema is just opposite (across the street)
Gíngchaat hái yahpbihn	The police are inside

A noun phrase can come between **hái** and the localizer, in the pattern **hái (. . .) X-mihn/bihn**:

Bún syū hái jēung tói seuhngbihn
(*lit.* the book on the table top)
The book is on the table

Kéuih kéih hái pō syuh hauhmihn
(*lit.* she stood at the tree behind)
She stood behind the tree

Ngóh jyuh hái kéuih ūkkéi deuimihn
(*lit.* I live at her home opposite)
I live opposite her (home)

douh 'there' serves colloquially as a localizer in this pattern:

A-Mā hái tēng douh	Mum's in the living room
Dī séung hái ngóh douh	The pictures are with me/at my place

While this pattern with two separate expressions of location may appear redundant, note that **douh** (or another localizer in its place) is required here:

Kéuihdeih hái ga chē douh	They're in the car
(not * **Kéuihdeih hái ga che**)	
Dī jīlíu hái dihnlóuh douh	The data are in the computer
(not * **Dī jīlíu hái dihnlóuh**)	

With **jīgāan** 'between', **tùhng** is used to join the two noun phrases concerned, in the pattern **X tùhng Y jīgāan**:

Ngóh tùhng kéuih jīgāan móuh saai gámchìhng
(*lit.* I and him between haven't all feeling)
There's no feeling left between us

Chìhnggám tùhng léihji jīgāan hóu làahn syúnjaahk
(*lit.* emotion and rationality between very hard to choose)
It's difficult to choose between emotion and rationality

(iii) A demonstrative form or localizer followed by the existential **yáuh** (or its negative counterpart **móuh**: Unit 6) or another verb:

Nīdouh yáuh hóu dō sailouhjái	There're many children here
Gódouh móuh yàuh-wìhng-chìh	There's no swimming pool there
Yahpbihn yáuh hóu dō yéh	There are lots of things inside
Hahbihn móuh chāantēng	Downstairs there's no restaurant
Chēutbihn lohk-gán yúh	It's raining outside

Again a noun phrase can be added before the localizer:

Daaihhohk léuihmihn yáuh sāam go tòuh-syū-gwún
There are three libraries in the university

Gāan fóng jūnggāan yáuh go gongkàhm
There's a piano in the middle of the room

Movement and direction

Movement towards a point in space may be expressed by **heung**:

Léih yīnggōi heung nībihn hàahng   You should walk this way
(or **Léih yīnggōi hàahng nībihn**)
Mhóu heung góbihn mohng   Don't look in that direction
(or **Mhóu mohng góbihn**)

To express a starting point in time or space, **yàuh** is used as follows:

Ngóh gāmyaht yàuh baat dím hōichí séuhng-tòhng
(*lit.* I today from eight o'clock beginning attended lessons)
Today I had classes from eight o'clock onwards

Yàuh Tòihwāan làih Hēunggóng yiu yāt go jūngtàuh fēigēi
(*lit.* from Taiwan coming to Hong Kong needs one hour's plane)
It's an hour's flight from Taiwan to Hong Kong

Yàuh nīdouh heui Syutlèih géi yúhn a?
(*lit.* from here go to Sydney how far)
How far is it from here to Sydney?

Note that the prepositional phrase comes before the verb.

yàuh is also used together with **dou** indicating the end point of a journey
in time or space:

Ngóhdeih yàuh gām jīu dáng dou yìhgā
We've been waiting from this morning till now

Yàuh daaihhohk dou ūkkéi yiu bun go jūng
It takes half an hour to get from the university to home

Kéuih yàuh sai dou daaih dōu haih gám ge
He's always been like this (*lit.* from small to big)

gīng 'via' introduces an intermediate step between the starting point and end point:

Ngóhdeih gīng Dūnggīng heui Sāam Fàahn Síh
(*lit.* we pass Tokyo go to San Francisco)
We're going to San Francisco via Tokyo

Léih hóyíh yàuh Hēunggóng dóu gīng seuihdouh dou ūkkéi
(*lit.* you can from Hong Kong island pass the tunnel arrive home)
You can go home from Hong Kong island via the tunnel

Reflecting the intermediate step in a journey, the phrase with **gīng** 'via' typically comes in the middle of the sentence, before the destination.
lèih is used to indicate distance from a location:

Yīyún lèih nīdouh géi yúhn a?
(*lit.* hospital from here how far)
How far is the hospital from here?

Ngóh ūkkéi lèih gēichèuhng yihsahp fānjūng
(*lit.* my home from the airport twenty minutes)
My home is twenty minutes from the airport

Note that a verb is not needed here.

Exercise 13.1

Express the location for each of the following using **hái** and a localizer in the spaces:

Example: **Dī fā** *hái* **fājēun** *yahpbihn*   The flowers are inside the vase

1 **Hohksāang** _____ **fóng** _____	The students are inside the room
2 **Jek māau** _____ **tói** _____	The cat is on the table
3 **Go jámtàuh** _____ **chòhng** _____	The pillow is on the bed
4 **Jī bāt** _____ **háp** _____	The pen is inside the box
5 **Bún syū** _____ **dang** _____	The book is under the chair
6 **Go jūng** _____ **chèuhng** _____	The clock is on the wall
7 **Bá jē** _____ **mùhn** _____	The umbrella is behind the door
8 **Dī séung** _____ **séungbóu** _____	The photos are inside the photo album
9 **Pō syuh** _____ **gāan ūk** _____	The tree is in front of the house
10 **Dihnsihgēi** _____ **syūgwaih** _____	The television is beside the bookcase

Exercise 13.2

Express the following in Cantonese:

1   behind the wall (**chèuhng**)
2   on top of the bookcase (**syūgwaih**)
3   opposite the bank (**ngàhnhòhng**)
4   in the middle of the road (**máhlouh**)
5   between the park (**gūngyún**) and the petrol station (**yàuh jaahm**)
6   sitting (**chóh**) beside you
7   inside the box (**háp**)
8   outside the classroom (**bāanfóng**)
9   in front of the mirror (**geng**)
10 below the table (**tói**)
11 towards this direction (**fōngheung**)
12 from morning (**jīu**) to evening (**máahn**)

Exercise 13.3

Say what there is at the following locations in your home:

1   On the table: **tói seuhngmihn** _____
2   On the wall: **chèuhng seuhngmihn** _____
3   In the kitchen: **chyùhfóng yahpbihn** _____
4   Inside the living room: **haak-tēng léuihmihn** _____
5   In the closet: **yīgwaih yahpbihn** _____
6   Under the bed: **chòhng hahmihn** _____
7   Under the chair: **dang hahbihn** _____
8   On the bookcase: **syūgwaih seuhngmihn** _____
9   In the bathroom: **sáisáu-gāan yahpbihn** _____
10 In the study: **syūfóng yahpbihn** _____

Exercise 13.4

Describe the following journeys:

   Example: from home to school: **yàuh ūkkéi heui hohkhaauh**

1   from here to the hospital (**yīyún**)
2   from the library (**tòuh-syū-gwún**) to the canteen (**faahn-tòhng**)
3   from the ground floor (**deih-há**) to the eighth floor (**baat láu**)
4   towards Kowloon (**Gáulùhng**)

5 to Tokyo (**Dūnggīng**) via Taipei (**Tòihbāk**)
6 from Hong Kong to London (**Lèuhndēun**) via Bangkok (**Maahn-gūk**)
7 from the study (**syūfóng**) to the kitchen (**chyùhfóng**)
8 from the first time (**daih yāt chi**) until now (**yìhgā**)
9 from the airport (**gēichèuhng**) to home (**ūkkéi**)
10 from the beginning (**tàuh**) to the end (**méih**)

UNIT FOURTEEN
Negation

To express negation, Cantonese uses negative words that all begin with the nasal consonant **m** and have low-register tones:

negative word		used with:
m̀h	not	adjectives, verbs referring to the present
móuh	have not	nouns, verbs referring to the past
meih	not yet	verbs
mhaih	is not	sentences
m-	un-	antonyms of adjectives and verbs

m̀h is used to negate:

(i) Most adjectives:

Nī gihn sāam m̀h pèhng ga	This shirt is not cheap
Dī jih m̀h chīngchó	The writing is not clear
Ngóh gīngyihm m̀h gau	My experience is not sufficient (*lit.* enough)

(ii) Verbs referring to the present:

Ngóh gāmyaht m̀h fāan-hohk	I'm not going to school today
Kéuihdeih m̀h sāu yihn-gām	They do not accept cash
Gūngsī jaahmsìh m̀h chéng yàhn	The company is not hiring anyone right now

móuh is the negative form of **yáuh** (Unit 6), used in two main ways:

(i) As a main verb:

Kéuih móuh làahm-pàhngyáuh ge	She doesn't have a boyfriend

| Ngóhdeih yìhgā móuh gūngyàhn | We don't have a (domestic) helper now |
| Ngóh móuh leng sāam jeuk | I have no nice clothes to wear |

(ii) As an auxiliary verb:

Ngóh gāmyaht móuh gin dóu kéuih a	I haven't seen her today
Kéuih móuh làih hōi-wúi	He didn't come to the meeting
Kéuihdeih móuh tūngjī ngóhdeih	They didn't inform us

móuh used in this way serves as the negative counterpart to **jó** (Unit 18), as can be seen in pairs like the following:

a	**Ngóh kàhmyaht máaih-jó choi**	I bought vegetables yesterday
b	**Ngóh kàhmyaht móuh máaih choi**	I didn't buy (any) vegetables yesterday
a	**Gūngsī chéng-jó kéuih**	The company has hired him
b	**Gūngsī móuh chéng kéuih**	The company has not hired him

meih as an auxiliary has the specific meaning 'not yet':

Ngóhdeih juhng meih būn ūk	We haven't moved house yet
Lóuhbáan meih fāan làih	The boss hasn't come in yet
Jaahmsìh meih yáuh sīusīk	So far there hasn't been any news

Attached to the end of a statement, **meih** makes a special form of question, typically with **jó** or **gwo** (see Unit 18):

Léih jouh-jó gūngfo meih a?
Have you done your homework (yet)?

Léih heui-gwo Hóiyèuhng Gūngyún meih a?
Have you ever been to Ocean Park?

mhaih 'it's not' is the negative form of the verb **haih** 'to be'. It is used in negating adjectives modified by an adverb (see Unit 9):

mhaih hóu leng	not very pretty
mhaih géi gūngpìhng	not quite fair
Ngóhdeih mhaih gam suhk	We're not that familiar (with each other)

Antonyms formed with negation

Antonyms of many adjectives (and some verbs) can be formed by adding a prefix **m-**:

hōisām	happy	→	**mhōisām**	unhappy
chīngchó	clear	→	**mchīngchó**	unclear
gūngpìhng	fair	→	**mgūngpìhng**	unfair
tùhngyi	agree	→	**mtùhngyi**	disagree

Some of these negative forms carry a meaning related to that of the underlying verb or adjective, but not simply its opposite:

gin	see	→	**mgin**	lose
geidāk	remember	→	**mgeidāk**	forget
tùhng	same	→	**mtùhng**	different
dākhàahn	at leisure	→	**mdākhàahn**	busy
syūfuhk	comfortable	→	**msyūfuhk**	unwell, sick

All such antonyms can be modified by **hóu** or other adverbs:

Kéuih *hóu* **mjūngyi léih ge tàihyíh**
She really dislikes your proposal

Gám yéung deui ngóh *taai* **mgūngpìhng**
(*lit.* this way towards me too unfair)
This is too unfair to me

A few such words exist in the negative form, i.e. they are inherently negative; without the prefix **m-**, they do not occur in an affirmative statement:

mhóuyisi	embarrassed
mfahnhei	discontented
Kéuih gokdāk hóu mhóuyisi	She feels very embarrassed
(but not *__Kéuih gokdāk hóu hóuyisi__)	
Ngóh gokdāk hóu mfahnhei	I feel very discontented
(but not *__Ngóh gokdāk hóu fahnhei__)	

Double negatives

Combinations of two negative forms are widely used to give a qualified or indirect positive meaning. A typical case is to use **mhaih** to deny a negative statement:

Ngóh mhaih m̀h seun léih	It's not that I don't believe you
Mhaih mhólàhng ge	It's not impossible
Ngóhdeih mhaih móuh hēimohng	We're not without hope (i.e. we still have a chance)

Another case involves negating both the main verb and an auxiliary (see Unit 20):

Kéuih m̀h wúih m̀h fāan làih	He won't fail to come back
Gám yéung m̀h wúih mgūngpìhng	That would not be unfair
Léih m̀h hóyíh m̀h béi chín	You cannot choose not to pay (i.e. you have to pay)

Exercise 14.1

Put these statements in the negative by using **móuh** or **mhaih**:

1 **Kéuih ūkkéi yáuh mahntàih**
   His family has problems
2 **Ngóhdeih hóu guih**
   We're very tired
3 **Ngóh sīng-jó-jīk**
   I got promoted
4 **Kéuih gihn sāam hóu gwai**
   Her dress is very expensive
5 **Ngóh tàuhsīn sihk-jó yeuhk**
   I have taken the medicine just now
6 **Yīsāng heui-jó douh-ga**
   The doctor has gone on holiday
7 **Lóuhbáan hóu lāu**
   The boss is very angry
8 **Dī hohksāang yáuh séuhng-móhng**
   The students have got on the Internet
9 **Dī hohksāang hóu kàhnlihk**
   The students are very diligent
10 **Gó tou hei taai chèuhng**
   That film is too long

Exercise 14.2

Show your disagreement with the following negative statements by providing the affirmative counterparts:

> Example: **Léih móuh sìhgaan** You have no time → **Ngóh yáuh sìhgaan (a)** I do have time (the particle **a** serves to soften the force of the disagreement, see Unit 25)

1 **Sihk hóisīn m̀h gwai**
   Eating seafood is not expensive
2 **Wòhng Sāang m̀h chéng kéuih**
   Mr Wong is not hiring her
3 **Léih móuh duhk-gwo Faatmán**
   You haven't studied French
4 **Kéuihdeih meih git-fān**
   They're not married
5 **Léih móuh bou-méng**
   You haven't applied
6 **Dī háausíh tàihmuhk mhaih hóu làahn**
   The exam questions are not very hard
7 **Gāan fóng m̀h gōnjehng**
   The room is not tidy
8 **Kéuih yìhgā mdākhàahn**
   He's busy now
9 **Gāmyaht móuh tòhng**
   There are no lessons today
10 **Ngóhdeih meih sihk-gwo sèh-gāng**
   We've never eaten snake soup

Exercise 14.3

Create antonyms based on the following adjectives and verbs, translate and pronounce them:

1	**sānsīn**	fresh	6	**jūngyi**	like
2	**síusām**	careful	7	**mìhngbaahk**	understand
3	**hóuchói**	lucky	8	**tùhngyi**	agree
4	**gōuhing**	glad	9	**yānséung**	appreciate
5	**gihnhōng**	healthy	10	**làuhsām**	attentive

† Exercise 14.4

A Create a double negative based on the sentence provided:

Example: **Ngóh m̀h séung heui** I don't want to go → **Ngóh mhaih m̀h séung heui**

1 **Kéuih móuh seunsām**	She lacks confidence
2 **Kéuih góng ge yéh móuh douhléih**	What he says is unreasonable
3 **Léih gājē m̀h wúih bōng léih**	Your sister won't help you
4 **Ngóhdeih m̀h gau chín**	We don't have enough money
5 **Léih gāmyaht mdākhàahn**	You're busy today

B Use a double negative to express the following indirectly:

Example: **Léih yātdihng yiu seun kéuih** You must believe him → **Léih m̀h hóyíh m̀h seun kéuih**

1 **Ngóhdeih tùhngyi**	We agree
2 **Ngóhdeih yiu jáu**	We must leave
3 **Gūngsī háng gā yàhn-gūng**	The company is willing to raise salaries
4 **Ngóh wúih geidāk**	I'll remember
5 **Léih máaih dāk héi**	You can afford it

UNIT FIFTEEN
Verbs of motion: **heui** and **làih**

The verbs **heui** 'go' and **làih** (or **lèih**) 'come' are used as follows:

(i) By themselves as main verbs:

Ngóhdeih yātchàih heui lā	Let's go together
Kéuih tīngyaht m̀h làih la	She's not coming tomorrow

Both can be followed directly by a place name or other expression of the destination, without a preposition as in English:

Ngóh yāt-yuht heui Méihgwok	I'm going to America in January
Ngóhdeih yìhgā heui fóchējaahm	We're going to the railway station now
Kéuihdeih m̀h làih Yīnggwok	They're not coming to England
Léih géisìh làih ngóh ūkkéi a?	When are you coming to my place?

They can also take a verb phrase to show the purpose of the journey:

heui (gwóng-chèuhng) yám-chàh	Go (to the shopping centre) for dim sum (*lit.* to drink tea)
làih (nīdouh) tái hei	Come (here) to see a film

(ii) Together with directional verbs:

yahp heui	go in	**yahp làih**	come in
chēut heui	go out	**chēut làih**	come out
séuhng heui	go up	**séuhng làih**	come up
lohk heui	go down	**lohk làih**	come down
gwo heui	go over	**gwo làih**	come over
fāan heui	go back	**fāan làih**	come back

These combinations are used in the same way as the simple verbs, for example:

Ngóh séuhng heui Bākgīng hōi-wúi
(*lit.* I ascend go Beijing hold meeting)
I'm going up to Beijing for a meeting

Ngóhdeih lohk heui sihk-faahn lā
(*lit.* we descend go eat rice)
Let's go down and eat

Léih géisìh gwo làih taam ngóh a?
(*lit.* you when over come visit me)
When are you coming over to visit me?

A third verb may be added before the directional verb to express the manner of movement, resulting in a sequence of three verbs: (manner – direction – come/go):

fēi yahp làih	fly in	**fēi chēut heui**	fly out
dit lohk làih	come falling down	**dit lohk heui**	go falling down
tiu séuhng làih	jump up (here)	**tiu séuhng heui**	jump up (there)
hàahng fāan làih	walk back (here)	**hàahng gwo heui**	walk over (there)

When used with a transitive verb, the directional verb and **heui/làih** follow the object:

Ngóhdeih séung daai dī sān tùhngsih yahp làih
(*lit.* we wish to bring some new colleagues in come)
We'd like to bring in some new colleagues

Ngóh līng dī hàhngléih séuhng làih sīn
(*lit.* I carry the luggage up come first)
I'll bring the luggage up first

Mgōi léih daih dī sung gwo làih
(*lit.* please you pass the food over come)
Could you pass the dishes over, please

Aspect markers like **jó** and **gán** (Units 18–19) appear after the first verb of the sequence:

Kéuihdeih chēut-jó heui hóu loih la	They've been out for a long time
Lóuhbáan fāan-gán làih ge la	The boss is on his way (*lit.* coming) back
Jek jeukjái fēi-jó yahp làih chyùhfóng	The bird has flown into the kitchen
Dī séui làuh-gán lohk heui hahmihn	The water is flowing downwards

These sequences of verbs are known as serial verb constructions. One such pattern, using both **làih** and **heui**, uses four verbs in a row:

hàahng làih hàahng heui	walk to and fro
fēi làih fēi heui	fly back and forth
lám làih lám heui	think it over and over
si làih si heui	try and try again

Directional verbs are also used as verbs in their own right, with a place expression as their object. This pattern includes a number of useful set phrases:

séuhng/lohk chē	get on/off a car, bus, etc.
séuhng/lohk sāan	go up/down a hill
yahp/chēut gíng	enter/leave a country (at the border)
yahp/chēut yún	enter/leave hospital
gwo máhlouh	cross the road
gwo hói	cross the sea, harbour, etc.
fāan ūkkéi	return home
fāan gūng	go (*lit.* return) to work

Exercise 15.1

Expand the sentence given by adding a directional verb:

Example: **heui Hēunggóng** go to Hong Kong → **gwo heui Hēunggóng** go over to Hong Kong/**fāan heui Hēunggóng** go back to Hong Kong

1	Làih ngóh ūkkéi	come to my place
2	Heui hohkhaauh	go to school
3	Heui làuhseuhng	go upstairs
4	Làih Yīnggwok	come to England
5	Heui séjihlàuh	go to the office
6	Làih tái-háh	come and take a look
7	Làih taam ngóhdeih	come to visit us
8	Heui hōi-wúi	go to a meeting

9 Làih sihk-faahn   come and eat
10 Heui jouh-yéh   go to work

Exercise 15.2

Add a suitable object to the verb sequences given to show the destination:

1 Ngóh tīngyaht heui _____   I'm going tomorrow
2 Léih làih _____ sihk-faahn   Come to eat
3 Ngóh gwo heui _____ wán yàhn   I'm going over to look for someone
4 Léih dākhàahn séuhng làih _____ Come up for a visit (*lit.* to sit)
   chóh   when you're free
5 Ngóhdeih yiu fēi fāan heui _____ We have to fly back
6 Go léuihjái jáu chēut heui _____ The girl ran out
7 Ngóh dī chānchīk fāan làih _____ My relatives are coming back for a
   douh-ga   holiday
8 Léih hóyīh lohk heui _____   You can go down to do some
   máaih yéh   shopping
9 Ngóh jīkhāak yahp heui _____   I'm going in to change right away
   wuhn sāam
10 Ngóh tùhngsih gwo làih _____   My colleague is coming over to
   kīng-gái   chat

Exercise 15.3

Fill in the blanks according to the translation:

1 _____ _____ Gáulùhng   Go over to Kowloon
2 _____ _____ ngóh gāan fóng Come into my room
3 _____ _____ Hēunggóng   Come down to Hong Kong (e.g
                                    from mainland China)
4 _____ _____ Bākgīng   Go up to Beijing
5 _____ _____ haak-tēng   Go out to the living room
6 _____ _____ ūkkéi   Come back home
7 Yàuh sahp láu dit _____ _____ Fall down from the tenth floor
8 Tiu _____ _____ ga fóchē   Jump onto the train
9 Hàahng _____ _____ syūfóng Walk into the study
10 Fēi _____ _____ Oujāu   Fly back to Australia

† Exercise 15.4

Add an aspect marker (**jó** or **gán**: see Units 18–19) in the appropriate place according to the English translation:

1	**Ga fochē fāan làih**	The lorry is coming back
2	**Dī seun gei heui Méihgwok**	The letters have been sent to the United States
3	**Dī gúpiu sīng séuhng heui gōu wái**	The shares have risen to a high
4	**Kéuih hái fóng hàahng chēut làih**	He's coming out of his room
5	**Kéuihdeih pàh séuhng làih sāandéng**	They're climbing up the top of the mountain
6	**Bún syū dit lohk heui deihhá**	The book has fallen down onto the floor
7	**Go kàhm būn gwo heui deuimihn**	The piano has been moved to the opposite side
8	**Ga chē hōi yahp làih tìhng-chē-chèuhng**	The car is driving into the car park
9	**Kéuih hàahng chēut heui gāai douh**	She's walking out onto the street
10	**Kéuihdeih būn lohk heui yih láu**	They're moving down to the second floor

UNIT SIXTEEN
Verbs of giving: **béi**

béi is an important verb used both on its own as a verb meaning 'give' and together with other verbs of giving. The verb **béi** takes two objects, the direct object (representing what is given) followed by the indirect object (representing the person to whom something is given):

Kéuih béi-jó yāt baak mān ngóh
(*lit.* she gave one hundred dollars me)
She gave me a hundred dollars

Ngóh béi-jó tìuh sósìh ngóh taaitáai
(*lit.* I gave the key my wife)
I gave my wife the key

Béi gān choi ngóh ā
(*lit.* give catty vegetables me)
Give me a catty of vegetables, please

Léih béi dī mín kéuih lā!
(*lit.* you give some face (to) her)
Show her some respect!

Note that the order of the two objects here is the reverse of that in English as well as that in Mandarin.

With other verbs of giving such as **gei** 'send' and **wàahn** 'return', **béi** 'to' is used to introduce the indirect object:

Ngóh pàhngyáuh gei-jó jēung kāat béi ngóh
My friend sent me a card

Ngóh yíhgīng wàahn-jó chín béi léih
I've already returned the money to you

Kéuih lóuhgūng làuh-jó gāan ūk béi kéuih
Her husband left her the house

Yáuh go yáuh-chín-lóu gyūn-jó hóu dō chín béi daaih-hohk
A rich man donated a lot of money to the university

Note here the verb **sung** which is used in this pattern to mean 'give' in the sense of giving presents:

Dī tùhngsih sung-jó dī fā béi kéuih
Her colleagues sent her some flowers

Kéuih lìhn-lìhn sung sāangyaht láihmaht béi ngóh go jái
She gives my son a birthday present every year

Nī jek gaaijí sung béi léih ge!
This ring is (a present) for you

A third verb may be added to the construction to indicate the purpose for which the object will be used:

Kéuih wúih gei dī màhn-gín béi léih chīm-méng
She will send the documents for you to sign

Go hohksāang chyùhnjān-jó pīn màhnjēung béi ngóh tái
The student faxed an article for me to read

Kéuih yiu jyú-faahn béi ūkkéi-yàhn sihk
She has to cook for her family (to eat)

béi **and permission**

béi can also indicate permission (allowing, letting someone do something):

Lóuhsī béi ngóhdeih jóu dī jáu	The teacher let us leave early
Ngóh béi léih yuhng ngóh go dihnlóuh	I'll let you use my computer
Mhóu béi yàhn jī a	Don't let anyone know

Other verbs with two objects

A number of other verbs can take two objects, such as **gaau** (teach), **mahn** (ask). Here the word order is different, with the indirect object coming first:

Kéuih gaau-gwo hóu dō yàhn gongkàhm
She has taught a lot of people the piano

Ngóh jūngyi mahn hohksāang mahntàih
I like to ask students questions

A similar pattern appears with verbs of deprivation such as **faht** (fine) and **tāu** (steal) or **chéung** (rob):

Gūngsī faht ngóhdeih géi baak mān
The company fined us a few hundred dollars

Ngóh yèhng-jó kéuih hóu dō chín
I won a lot of money from him

Yáuh go cháak tāu-jó ngóh sāam bún syū
A thief has stolen three books from me

Kàhm máahn yáuh yàhn chéung kéuih yéh
Last night someone robbed things from him

The verb **je** when used in this pattern can be ambiguous, meaning either 'lend' or 'borrow' according to the context:

    Ngóh je-jó kéuih yāt baak mān
    I borrowed $100 from him
or I lent him $100

    Ngóh gājē je-jó ngóh géi tiuh kwàhn
    My sister has borrowed a few dresses from me
or My sister has lent me a few dresses

To make the meaning clear, the preposition **tùhng** or **heung** can be used to mean 'borrow from':

    Ngóh tùhng kéuih jē-jó yāt baak mān   I borrowed $100 from him
or **Ngóh heung kéuih jē-jó yāt baak mān**

By contrast, using **béi** to introduce the indirect object gives the meaning 'lend':

Ngóh je-jó yāt baak mān béi kéuih   I lent him $100
Ngóh gājē je-jó géi tiuh kwàhn béi ngóh My sister has lent me a
                                          few dresses

Exercise 16.1

Add an indirect object to show who the object is given to:

1	**Ngóh yiu béi chín**	I have to pay (money)
2	**Léih yiu wàahn syū**	You need to return some books
3	**Ngóh séung sung láihmaht**	I want to give a present
4	**Ngóh heui gei seun**	I'm going to send a letter
5	**Faai dī dá-dihnwá**	Hurry up and call (telephone)
6	**Léih tīngyaht gāau gūngfo**	Hand in your homework tomorrow
7	**Mgōi léih làuh sung**	Please leave some food (for someone to eat)
8	**Ngóh sèhngyaht máaih sāam**	I'm always buying clothes (for someone to wear)
9	**Ngóh hóyíh gáan tou hei**	I can pick a film (for someone to watch)
10	**Ngóh séung dím gō**	I'd like to request a song (for someone to listen to)

Exercise 16.2

Translate the following sentences using appropriate verbs of giving:

1 He gave me some perfume (**dī hēungséui**)
2 The doctor (**yīsāng**) gave me some medicine (**dī yeuhk**)
3 I'm going to return the documents (**dī màhn-gín**) to you
4 The boss (**lóuhbáan**) donated a lot of money to the church (**gaauwúi**)
5 He sent his family (**ūkkéi-yàhn**) a letter (**fūng seun**)
6 I lent him a pencil (**jī yùhnbāt**)
7 Please give him face (respect: **mín**)
8 You must give me back the key (**tiuh sósìh**)
9 He wants to borrow two books (**léuhng bún syū**) from me
10 The lecturer (**go góngsī**) gave us some homework (**gūngfo**) to do

Exercise 16.3

Add an indirect object to show the recipient of the action:

Example: **Ngóh sīk gaau gongkàhm** I know how to teach the piano
→ **Ngóh sīk gaau daaih-yàhn gongkàhm** I know how to teach adults the piano

1	**Ngóhdeih juhng yiu béi chín**	We still have to pay (money)
2	**Ngóh gājē je-jó hóu dō sāam**	My sister lent a lot of clothes
3	**Gó go yàhn sèhngyaht tāu yéh**	That person is always stealing things
4	**Yáuh yàhn chéung-jó hóu dō chín**	Somebody has stolen a lot of money
5	**Ngóh heui je géi bún syū**	I'm going to borrow a few books
6	**Kéuih séung mahn géi yeuhng yéh**	She wants to ask a few things
7	**Ngóh go pàhngyáuh gaau Yīngmán ge**	My friend teaches English
8	**Jingfú wúih faht chín ge**	The government will impose a fine

UNIT SEVENTEEN
Verbs and particles

The Cantonese verb combines with a rich, versatile set of particles (also known as verbal complements). The resulting combinations often resemble those known as verb-particle constructions (or phrasal verbs) in English, as in the following cases:

tiu héi	jump up	**tiu gwo**	jump over
báai dāi	put down	**báai fāan**	put back

The particles may indicate the state of an object as the result of an action, or different phases of an action (beginning, continuing or ending). According to the functions they serve, they can be divided into the following categories:

1 Directional particles, indicating the direction of movement or action:

yahp	in	**máaih**	buy + **yahp**	→ **máaih yahp**	buy in, acquire
chēut	out	**gei**	send + **chēut**	→ **gei chēut**	send out
héi	up	**gwa**	hang + **héi**	→ **gwa héi**	hang up (clothes, etc.)
dāi	down	**fong**	put + **dāi**	→ **fong dāi**	put down
fāan	back	**ló**	bring + **fāan**	→ **ló fāan**	bring back
gwo	over, past	**gīng**	pass + **gwo**	→ **gīng gwo**	pass by
hōi	away	**hàahng**	walk + **hōi**	→ **hàahng hōi**	walk away, step out
màaih	closer	**hàahng**	walk + **màaih**	→ **hàahng màaih**	come closer

Note that some of these items (**yahp, chēut, fāan** and **gwo**) are the same as the directional verbs introduced in Unit 15. The meaning of the combinations is often predictable, as in the above examples, but it can also be figurative or quite idiomatic as in the following cases:

héi	up	**Lóuhbáan hóu tái héi kéuih** The boss has a high opinion of him **Ngóh juhng meih jouh héi gūngfo** I haven't finished my homework
fāan	back	**Kéuih yìhgā jouh fāan gíngchaat** He's gone back to being a policeman **Ngóh séung máaih fāan dī leng sāam** I want to buy myself some nice clothes
gwo	over	**Léih jeui hóu sé gwo pīn mán** You'd better rewrite (write over) the essay **Ngóh hah chi sīn tùhng léih wáan gwo** I'll play with you again next time

2 Resultative particles, describing the extent or consequences of an action:

báau	full up	**sihk** → **sihk báau**	eat + **báau** eat one's full share
cho	wrongly	**gáan** → **gáan cho**	choose + **cho** make the wrong choice
dihm	conclusively	**gáau** → **gáau dihm**	manage + **dihm** deal with
dihng	ready	**lám** → **lám dihng**	think + **dihng** think in advance
dóu	accomplish	**sāu** → **sāu dóu**	collect + **dóu** receive
dou	arrive	**heui** → **heui dou**	go + **dou** arrive
hóu	complete	**jouh** → **jouh hóu**	do + **hóu** finish up (doing)
jihng	remain	**sihk** → **sihk jihng**	eat + **jihng** leave behind (after eating)
mìhng	clear	**sé** → **sé mìhng**	write + **mìhng** put in writing
séi	to death	**muhn** → **muhn séi**	bored + **séi** (be) bore(d) to death
sèhng	succeed	**jouh** → **jouh sèhng**	do + **sèhng** complete (a deal, etc.)
waaih	bad, broken	**gaau** → **gaau waaih**	teach + **waaih** lead astray
yùhn	to the end	**tái** → **tái yùhn**	read + **yùhn** finish reading

Verbs of perception

An important sub-type of verb + particle construction involves verbs of perception. In these combinations, a verb denoting some mode of perception combines with the particle **dóu** to indicate successful perception of an object:

tēng	listen	→	**tēng dóu**	hear
tái	look, watch, read	→	**tái dóu**	see
gin	see, meet	→	**gin dóu**	see, notice
wán	seek, look for	→	**wán dóu**	find
màhn	smell	→	**màhn dóu**	smell (something)
lám	think (about)	→	**lám dóu**	think of (a problem, solution, etc.)
gám gok	feeling	→	**gok dóu, gám gok dóu**	feel (something)

The simple verbs on the left describe activities, the combinations with **dóu** successful perception:

tēng gō	listen to songs	**tēng dóu sēng**	hear a noise
tái sānmán	watch the news	**tái dóu bougou**	see a report
lám baahnfaat	(try to) think of a way		
lám dóu go baahnfaat	think of a way		

Potential constructions

Verb-particle combinations can be separated by **m̀h** and **dāk** in constructions which express inability and potential respectively:

heui m̀h dóu	cannot get there
heui dāk dóu	can get there
tái m̀h dóu	cannot see
tái (dāk) dóu	can see
tēng m̀h chēut	cannot tell
tēng dāk chēut	can tell (by listening)
tēng m̀h mìhng	cannot understand
tēng dāk mìhng	can understand (what one hears)

Some examples:

Ngóhdeih tái m̀h dóu go dihnyíng mìhngsīng
We could not see the film star

Ngóh tēng dāk mìhng léih ge Gwóngdūng-wá
I can understand your Cantonese

Ngóh tēng dāk chēut léih haih Méihgwokyàhn
I can tell (by listening) that you're American

Ngóh lám m̀h héi kéuih go Yīngmàhn méng
I cannot think of his English name

Such combinations often have idiomatic meanings:

seun m̀h gwo	cannot trust	**seun dāk gwo**	can trust
máaih m̀h héi	cannot afford	**máaih dāk héi**	can afford
díng m̀h seuhn	cannot stand	**díng dāk seuhn**	can stand
gón m̀h chit	cannot make it (in time)	**gón dāk chit**	can make it (in time)

Exercise 17.1

Add a particle after the verb from the list provided:

(cho, dāi, dou, dóu, fāan, gwo, hōi, yùhn)

1	**tái** _____ **ga chē**	see the car
2	**báai** _____ **gihn sāam**	put the dress down
3	**ló** _____ **dī seun**	bring back the mail (letters)
4	**gīng** _____ **yīyún**	pass by the hospital
5	**lám** _____ **baahnfaat**	think of a solution
6	**tái** _____ **boují**	finish reading the newspaper
7	**yihng** _____ **yàhn**	misrecognize someone
8	**jáu** _____	go away
9	**sāu** _____ **chín**	receive money
10	**heui** _____ **gūngsī**	arrive at the office

Exercise 17.2

Translate the following using verbs of perception:

1 He often listens to stories (**gújái**)
2 I hear rumours (**yìuhyìhn**)
3 He's already thought of the answer (**go daahp-on**)
4 I saw an advertisement (**go gwónggou**)

5 You can feel the pressure (**ngaatlihk**)
6 I smell smoke (**yīnmeih**)
7 She likes to read novels (**síusyut**)
8 She doesn't like watching films (**hei**)

Exercise 17.3

Express the following situations using **m̀h** and the particle **dóu**:

Example: You cannot see (your name) → **Ngóh tái m̀h dóu (ngóh go méng)**

1   You did not receive her letter (**kéuih fūng seun**)
2   You cannot buy the cinema ticket (**hei fēi**)
3   You could not see the sign (**go páai**)
4   You cannot smell the food (**dī sung**)
5   You cannot hear the aeroplanes (**fēigēi sēng**)
6   You cannot think of how to answer (**dím daap**)
7   You cannot remember (**gei**) so many names (**gam dō méng**)
8   You cannot eat so much ice cream (**gam dō syutgōu**)
9   You cannot find (**wán**) a letter (**fūng seun**)
10 Your friend cannot get (**heui**) to Shatin

Exercise 17.4

Use the potential **dāk** to contradict the following statements:

Example: **Ngóhdeih heui m̀h dóu Bālàih** We cannot get to Paris → **heui dāk dóu** Yes we can (Note that this response is sufficient: there is no need to repeat the subject or object.)

1 **Kéuih béi m̀h dóu ōnchyùhn-gám ngóh**	He can't give me a sense of security
2 **Ngóh gáau m̀h dihm léuhng go sailouh**	I can't deal with two kids
3 **Gām máahn tái m̀h dóu sīng-sīng**	We can't see the stars tonight
4 **Nī dāan sāangyi jouh m̀h sèhng**	We cannot complete the deal
5 **Kéuihdeih seun m̀h gwo ga**	They can't be trusted
6 **Léih saht máaih m̀h héi**	I bet you can't afford it
7 **Gām chi ngóhdeih jouh m̀h chit**	This time we won't manage it in time
8 **Léih tēng m̀h mìhng ngóh ge Jūngmán àh?**	Can't you understand my Chinese?

UNIT EIGHTEEN
Actions and events: jó and gwo

Cantonese is said to lack tense, in the sense that the form taken by the verb does not consistently indicate the location of events in time. We have already seen how adverbs can serve to indicate when events take place (Unit 11); in this unit we introduce the aspect markers **jó** and **gwo** which also play an important role here. Although it may be tempting to equate **jó** and/or **gwo** with past tense, the fact of referring to the past is neither a necessary nor a sufficient condition for their use. They are termed aspect markers because they are concerned with the way an action is viewed – as complete, or as ongoing as discussed in Unit 19 – rather than directly with time.

Perfective jó

A sentence can refer to the past merely by including an adverb such as **yíhchìhn** 'before' (Unit 11):

Ngóhdeih yíhchìhn hái Gānàhdaaih jyuh ge
We lived in Canada before

By adding the perfective suffix **jó** to the verb it is possible to refer to the same situation as a complete whole:

Ngóhdeih hái Gānàhdaaih jyuh-jó sāam lìhn
We lived in Canada for three years

In this case specifying the period of three years, now completed, calls for the suffix **jó**. Adverbs such as **yíhgīng** 'already', **ngāam-ngāam** 'just' and **tàuhsīn** 'just now' also favour **jó**:

Kéuih yíhgīng kyutdihng-jó chìhjīk
He has already decided to resign

Kéuihdeih ngāam-ngāam lèih-jó-fān
They've just had a divorce

Ngóh tàuhsīn daap-jó léih ge mahntàih
I answered your question just now

Naturally this tends to place the action in the past. It also extends to a period of time up to and including the present:

Ngóh taaitáai gaau-jó sāam lìhn Yīngmán
My wife has taught/has been teaching English for three years

Ngóh tái-jó bun yaht syū
I have been reading for half a day

Ngóh sailóu jouh-jó gíngchaat hóu loih
My brother has been a policeman for a long time

Experiential gwo

The 'experiential' meaning of **gwo** corresponds to one of the meanings of the present perfect in English – that something has happened at least once. Given a human subject, this is essentially the concept of experience, hence the grammatical term 'experiential' to describe this function. Typical cases are:

Léih yáuh-móuh sihk-gwo Góngsīk sāi chāan a?
Have you eaten Hong Kong-style western food?

Léih heui-gwo Taai-hūng Gwún meih a?
Have you been to the Space Museum?

Adverbs which call for **gwo** include **chàhnggīng** 'once' and **meih** 'not yet':

Kéuih chàhnggīng oi-gwo ngóh	She once loved me
Ngóh meih yám-gwo nī jek jáu	I've not drunk this wine before
(not * **Ngóh meih yám-jó nī jek jáu**)	

jó versus gwo

jó and gwo may appear similar in meaning, both corresponding to the present perfect forms of the verb in English. Indeed there will be cases when either makes sense:

Ngóh tái-jó sāam go yīsāng	I've (just) seen three doctors
Ngóh tái-gwo sāam go yīsāng	I've seen three doctors (before)
Kéuih sé-jó yāt pīn mán	He's (just) written an article
Kéuih sé-gwo yāt pīn mán	He's written an article (before)
Kéuih jyuh-jó sāam go yuht yīyún	He's been in hospital for three months (recently)
Kéuih jyuh-gwo sāam go yuht yīyún	He's been in hospital for three months (once before)
Ngóh wán-jó léih géi chi	I've looked for you several times (recently)
Ngóh wán-gwo léih géi chi	I've looked for you several times (before)

In such cases, jó puts a focus on the result or current relevance of the action, while gwo makes it of less immediate relevance:

Ngóh máaih-jó nī jek pàaihjí
I've bought this brand (and still have it)

Ngóh máaih-gwo nī jek pàaihjí
I've bought this brand (before, in the past)

Kéuih heui-jó gēichèuhng
He's gone to the airport (and is still there or on his way)

Kéuih heui-gwo gēichèuhng
He's been to the airport (but is no longer there)

Questions with meih

Statements with either jó or gwo can be turned into yes/no questions by adding meih (see also Unit 23).

Léih sīk-jó dāng meih a?	Have you turned the light(s) off?
Léih si-gwo nī júng hēungséui meih a?	Have you tried this perfume before?

Such questions are answered by the verb + **jó** or **gwo**:

A: **Léih chūng-jó-lèuhng meih a?** Have you taken a bath yet?
B: **Chūng-jó la/meih a** Yes/no
A: **Léih si-gwo nī dī meih a?** Have you ever tried these?
B: **Si-gwo la/meih (si-gwo) a** Yes/no

Negating jó and gwo

Because it suggests completion of an action, **jó** is not compatible with negation. The negative counterpart of **jó** is **móuh** (have not) or **meih** (not yet):

Kéuih yīngsìhng-jó ngóh	He (has) promised me
Kéuih móuh yīngsìhng ngóh	He didn't promise me
(not * **Kéuih móuh yīngsìhng-jó ngóh**)	
Kéuih meih yīngsìhng ngóh	He hasn't promised me yet
(not * **Kéuih meih yīngsìhng-jó ngóh**)	
Ngóhdeih sihk-jó-faahn	We've had our dinner
Ngóhdeih meih sihk-faahn	We haven't had dinner yet
(not * **Ngóhdeih meih sihk-jó-faahn**)	

Unlike **jó**, **gwo** can be negated either with **móuh** or **meih**:

Ngóh móuh sāu-gwo léih ge chín	I have not received your money
Kéuih meih jouh-gwo sáuseuht	She has not yet had an operation

Exercise 18.1

Choose **jó** or **gwo** to fill in the gaps:

1 **Ngóh gin _____ kéuih ūkkéi yàhn** I've met his family before
2 **Ngóh tàuhsīn sái _____ tàuh** I've just washed my hair
3 **Kéuih gāmjīu sihk _____ jóuchāan la** He had breakfast this morning
4 **Ngóh tēng _____ nī sáu gō** I've heard this song before
5 **Ngóh heui _____ yāt chi Bākgīng** I've been to Beijing once
6 **Ngóh bou _____ méng hohk yàuhséui** I've applied for swimming lessons
7 **Kéuih yèhng _____ tàuh jéung** She's won the first prize!
8 **Kéuih meih háau _____ daih yāt mìhng** She hasn't got first place in an exam before
9 **Kéuih meih máaih _____ sān chē** He hasn't bought a new car before

10   Ngóh ngāam-ngāam maaih _____   I just sold the car
     ga chē

Exercise 18.2

Add **jó** or **gwo** to the following questions in accordance with the translation:

1   **Léih lám _____ yìhmàhn meih a?**   Have you ever considered
                                                emigrating?
2   **Go bìhbī fan _____ meih a?**   Has the baby gone to sleep yet?
3   **Léih si _____ nī jek yeuhk meih a?** Have you tried this medicine
                                                before?
4   **Léih yeuk _____ kéuih meih a?**   Have you made an appointment
                                                with him yet?
5   **Léih sānchíng _____ gó fahn gūng**   Have you applied for that job
     meih a?   yet?
6   **Ga chē johng _____ meih a?**   Has the car ever had an
                                                accident?
7   **Bún syū chēutbáan _____ meih a?**   Has the book been published
                                                yet?
8   **Léih cheung _____ nī sáu gō meih a?** Have you sung this song before?
9   **Léih gāmjīu tái _____ boují meih a?** Have you read the newspaper
                                                this morning?
10 **Lóuhbáan fāan _____ ūkkéi meih a?**   Has the boss gone home yet?

Exercise 18.3

Negate the following sentences (refer to Unit 14 if necessary):

Example: **Kéuihdeih git-jó-fān** They've got married: **Kéuihdeih móuh git-fān** (They have not got married) or **Kéuihdeih meih git fān** (They're not married yet)

1   **Dī hohksāang jáu-jó**   The students have gone
2   **Ngóh go jái heui-gwo Yīnggwok**   My son has been to England
3   **Kéuih ló-jó chēpàaih**   She's got her driving licence
4   **Ngóhdeih jouh-gwo jingfú gūng**   We've worked for the government
                                         before
5   **Ngóh dehng-jó fóng**   I've reserved a room
6   **Go beisyū fong-jó ga**   The secretary has taken a day off
7   **Ngóh yám-gwo Chīngdóu bējáu**   I've drunk Tsingtao beer before
8   **Ngóh tùhng kéuih paak-gwo-tō**   I've been on a date with him

9 **Dihnfai gā-jó ga**   Electricity costs have gone up
10 **Lóuhbáan laauh-gwo kéuih**   The boss has scolded him before

Exercise 18.4

Choose an appropriate adverb to add to each sentence from the list (a-f):

1 **Kéuih meih si-gwo chìh dou**   a **yíhgīng**   already
   She's never been late
2 **Ngóhdeih heui-gwo léih ūkkéi**   b **ngāam-ngāam**   just
   We've been to your house
3 **Ngóh sīnsāang fāan-jó séjihlàuh** c **chàhngging**   once
   My husband has gone to the office
4 **Kéuih sāang-jó go jái**   d **yíhchìhn**   before
   She's had a child
5 **Ngóh háauleuih-gwo chìhjīk**   e **jeuigahn**   recently
   I've considered resigning
6 **Gāan jáulàuh sāan-jó mùhn**   f **chùhnglòih**   never
   The restaurant has closed

UNIT NINETEEN
Activities: **gán** and **jyuh**

The aspect markers **gán** and **jyuh** attached to verbs express ongoing actions.

1 Progressive gán and háidouh

The progressive suffix **-gán**, like the English progressive '-ing', is used for ongoing activities:

Kéuih yìhgā hōi-gán-wúi She's having a meeting
Kéuihdeih léuhng go kīng-gán-gái The two of them are chatting

Unlike the English '-ing' in such cases, **gán** does not have to be present. Thus the same sentences shown above are also possible without **gán** (although a sentence particle may be needed in its place: see Unit 25):

Kéuih yìhgā hōi-wúi wo She's having a meeting
Kéuihdeih léuhng go kīng-gái la The two of them are chatting

Although referring most often to the present, verbs with **gán** may apply to an activity in the past. In such cases there is typically a past time adverb present to make this clear (see Unit 11; note also the adverb **juhng** 'still'):

Gauh lín kéuih juhng duhk-gán jūnghohk
Last year she was still studying in secondary school

Kéuihdeih seuhng go yuht juhng paak-gán-tō, yìhgā yíhgīng fān-jó-sáu la
Last month they were still dating, now they're already separated

Similarly, **gán** may be used in subordinate clauses referring to the past:

Ngóh duhk-gán síuhohk gójahnsìh, kéuih yíhgīng sīk ngóh
(*lit.* I studying primary school that time, he already knew me)
When I was in primary school, she already knew me

Léih fan-gán-gaau gójahnsìh, yáuh yàhn dá-dihnwá làih
(*lit.* you sleeping that time, somebody telephoned come)
Somebody called while you were sleeping

An alternative means of describing an ongoing action is by using **háidouh**, which literally means 'to be here/there':

Ngóh háidouh jouh gūngfo	I'm (here) doing homework
Léih háidouh dáng bīngo a?	Who are you waiting for?
Kéuihdeih háidouh aai-gāau	They're having an argument

Because of the literal meaning 'here', it is suitable where the activity is going on in a location close to the speaker. **háidouh** and **gán** can also be used together in expressing progressive meaning:

Kéuih háidouh jyú-gán-faahn	She's cooking
Lóuhbáan háidouh sé-gán-seun	The boss is writing letters

2 Continuous jyuh

jyuh added to a verb describes a continuous activity or state without change. It is associated with particular verbs, such as those denoting stationary situations:

Ga dihndāanchē jó-jyuh go chēutháu
The motorbike is blocking the exit

Kéuih sèhngyaht jā-jyuh fahn boují
She's always holding a newspaper

Ngóh yaht-yaht deui-jyuh tùhng-yéung yāt bāan yàhn
I face the same bunch of people every day

Certain transitive verbs with **jyuh** indicate putting something in a state, as with **kám-jyuh** 'cover' and **bóng-jyuh** 'tie up':

Léih yiu yuhng go goi kám-jyuh go wok
You need to use the top to cover the wok

Kéuih yuhng dī hóu leng ge jí bāau-jyuh fahn láihmaht
She used some nice paper to wrap up the gift

Kéuih móuh baahnfaat bóng-jyuh kéuih lóuhgūng
There's no way she can tie up her husband (physically or
  metaphorically)

Note that verb + **jyuh** can mean something different from the simple verb
by itself, such as **lám-jyuh** 'intend' vs. **lám** 'think', **tái-jyuh** 'watch over'
vs. **tái** 'look, see':

Ngóh lám-jyuh chéng kéuihdeih sihk-faahn
I intend to invite them to dinner

Léih tái-jyuh nī léuhng go sailouhjái, mhóu béi kéuihdeih dá-gāau
Keep an eye on these two kids, (and) don't let them fight

A verb with **jyuh** can also be used to describe an action carried out simultaneously with another:

Kéuih mohng-jyuh ngóh siu
(*lit.* he watching me smiled)
He smiled (while looking) at me

Kéuih deui-jyuh ngóh haam
(*lit.* she facing me cried)
She cried at (while facing) me

Léih gān-jyuh ngóh hàahng
(*lit.* you following me walk)
Walk after (following) me

Note that there is no conjunction linking the two verbs (this is a characteristic of the sequences of verb phrases known as serial verb constructions).

gán **versus** jyuh

Since both may be translated with progressive '-ing' foms in English, it
can be difficult to choose between **gán** and **jyuh**. As a general rule, **gán**
is appropriate for activities involving change or movement and **jyuh** for
static ones. In some cases either is possible, sometimes with a marked
difference of meaning:

a	**Kéuih ló-gán dī wuhn-geuih**	He's fetching the toys
b	**Kéuih ló-jyuh dī wuhn-geuih**	He's holding the toys
a	**Kéuih jeuk-gán sāam**	She's getting dressed
b	**Kéuih jeuk-jyuh tìuh dyún kwàhn**	She was wearing a short skirt
a	**Kéuih daai-gán tìuh jyunsehk génglín**	She's putting on a diamond necklace
b	**Kéuih daai-jyuh tìuh jyunsehk génglín**	She's wearing a diamond necklace

In each case **gán** indicates a dynamic, changing situation and **jyuh** a static one.

Exercise 19.1

Add **gán** and/or **háidouh** to express progressive aspect in the following sentences:

Example: **Kéuih tái syū** She's reading (a book) → **Kéuih tái-gán syū**

1	**Ngóh yìhgā wuhn sāam**	I'm changing (my clothes) now
2	**Kéuihdeih kàhm-máahn dá màhjéuk**	They were playing mahjong last night
3	**Kéuih góng dihnwá**	She's (talking) on the phone
4	**Yìhgā lohk yúh**	It's raining now
5	**Dī sailouhjái wáan séui**	The children are playing water games
6	**Ngóhdeih hàahng làih**	We're coming (walking) over
7	**Kéuih yìhgā chūng-lèuhng**	She's taking a shower
8	**Ngóh go jái waahk-wá**	My son is drawing
9	**Lóuhbáan hōi-wúi**	The boss is having a meeting
10	**Kéuih juhng lāu ngóhdeih**	She's still angry with us

Exercise 19.2

Add **gán** or **jyuh** as appropriate to complete the following sentences:

Example: **Ngóh sái sāam** I'm washing clothes → **Ngóh sái-gán sāam**

1	**Ngóh jā tìuh sósìh**	I'm holding a key
2	**Kéuih máaih sung**	She is buying groceries
3	**Ngóhdeih hóu gwa léih**	We miss you very much
4	**Léih jyú mātyéh a?**	What are you cooking?
5	**Kéuih yám gafē**	He's drinking coffee

6 **Dímgáai léih mohng ngóh a?**	Why are you staring at me?
7 **Dī sailouhjái chūng-lèuhng**	The children are taking a bath
8 **Hóu dō yàhn wán gūng**	Many people are looking for a job
9 **Ngóh yìhgā daap mahntàih**	I'm answering questions right now
10 **Kéuih sèhngyaht jeuk dī gauh sāam**	He's always wearing old clothes

Exercise 19.3

Add **jyuh** and the verb provided to expand the following sentences:

Example: **Léih gān ngóh** Follow me,
(**cheung** 'sing') → **Léih gān-jyuh ngóh cheung** Sing along with me

1 **Kéuih jeuk sāam**
   He wears clothes (**yàuh-séui** 'swim')
2 **Kéuih līng dī hàhngléih**
   He carried the baggage (**jáu** 'leave')
3 **Kéuih tái dihnsih**
   She's watching television (**jouh gūngfo** 'do homework')
4 **Dímgáai léih m̀h mohng ngóh?**
   Why aren't you looking at me (**góng** 'speak')?
5 **Ngóh jūngyi tēng yāmngohk**
   I like to listen to music (**yāusīk** 'relax')
6 **Kéuih sèhngyaht chī léih go léui**
   He's always hanging around your daughter (**heui gāai** 'go out')
7 **Go māmìh póuh go jái**
   The mother is carrying her son (**chēut gāai** 'go out')
8 **Dímgáai léih daai ngáahn-gēng?**
   Why do you wear your glasses? (**fan-gaau** 'sleep')
9 **Ngóh lóuhgūng jā ga sān chē**
   My husband is driving his new car (**làih jip ngóh** 'to meet me')
10 **Ngóh m̀h wúih jó léih**
   I won't get in your way (**faat daaht** 'make money')

UNIT TWENTY
Auxiliary verbs

Auxiliary verbs are used together with a main verb. The most important auxiliary verbs are:

wúih	will, would	**yīnggōi**	should, ought to
hóyíh	can, may	**yiu, sēuiyiu**	want, need
sīk	know (how to)	**séung**	want to

They express mainly 'modal' meanings having to do with possibility and necessity. The auxiliary verbs come before the main verb:

Ngóh wúih sé seun béi léih	I'll write to you
Léih yīnggōi douh-hip	You should apologise
Kéuih sīk góng Faatmán	He can speak French

An adverb may intervene between auxiliary and verb, as in the following examples:

Léih hóyíh *sīn* heui Jūngwàahn	You can go to Central *first*
Ngóh yīnggōi *dō dī* wanduhng	I should exercise *more*
Ngóhdeih séung *faai dī* bātyihp	We want to graduate *quickly*

Note that some of the auxiliary verbs double as main verbs:

Main verb		Auxiliary	
sīk	to know (someone)	**sīk**	to know (how to do something)
yiu	to want (something, someone)	**yiu**	to need (to do)

Compare the meanings in the following:

Ngóh sīk kéuih	I know her
Ngóh sīk yàuh-séui	I know how to swim
Kéuih yiu gafē	She wants coffee
Kéuih yiu sihk-yéh	She wants/needs to eat

A rare irregularity should be noted here. The form **m̀h yiu** means 'don't want', usually as a main verb:

| Ngóh m̀h yiu tìhmbán, mgōi | I don't want any dessert, thanks |
| Kéuih m̀h yiu daap fēigēi | He doesn't want to take the plane |

However, the negative form of **yiu** used as an auxiliary meaning 'need' is not **m̀h yiu** but **msái**:

	Ngóh gāmyaht yiu fāan gūng	I need to go to work today
but	Ngóh gāmyaht msái fāan gūng	I don't need to go to work today
	Kéuih yiu tái yīsāng	He needs to see the doctor
but	Kéuih msái tái yīsāng	He doesn't need to see the doctor

sēuiyiu is a more explicit form of **yiu**:

| Ngóhdeih sēuiyiu dō dī yāusīk | We need to rest more |
| Léih m̀h sēuiyiu gam sām-gāp | You needn't be so impatient |

háng 'to be willing' is used mainly (though not exclusively) in the negative form **m̀h háng**:

Ngóh go jái m̀h háng fāan hohk	My son won't go to school
Kéuih m̀h háng tēng ngóh dihnwá	She won't answer my calls
Ngóh gājē háng bōng sáu	My (elder) sister is willing to help

Modal meanings

Since Cantonese does not have a grammatical category of tense, **wúih** should not be thought of simply as a future tense. Rather, **wúih** has a range of meanings including future ('will') and conditional ('would'):

| Ngóh tīngyaht wúih làih | I'll come tomorrow |
| Ngóh m̀h wúih bōng kéuih | I wouldn't help him |

The basic modal meanings can be modified by modal adverbs such as **waahkjé** and **hólàhng** 'perhaps', **hángdihng** and **yātdihng** 'certainly':

Kéuihdeih waahkjé wúih yìhmàhn	They may (perhaps) emigrate
Kéuihdeih hángdihng wúih yìhmàhn	They will definitely emigrate
Ngóh hólàhng wúih jouh	I may do it
Ngóh yātdihng wúih jouh	I will certainly do it

Note here the distinction between **yātdihng yiu** meaning 'must' in the sense of obligation and **yātdihng haih** in the sense of logical necessity or inference:

Léih yātdihng yiu làih	You really must come
Léih yātdihng haih jyūn-gā	You must be an expert
Kéuih yātdihng yiu jouh ge	He must (has to) do it
Yātdihng haih kéuih jouh ge	It must have been him (who did it)

Since **haih** is not used with adjectives (Unit 9), **yātdihng** alone indicates inference with an adjective:

Léih yātdihng hóu guih	You must be tired
Léih go léui yātdihng hóu lēk ge	Your daughter must be pretty smart

yīnggōi can mean 'should' in the sense of either obligation or probability:

Léih yīnggōi jéunsìh fāan gūng
You should get to work on time

Léih fahn láihmaht yīnggōi jéunsìh dou
Your present should arrive on time (I expect)

Kéuih gāmyaht yīnggōi fāan làih ge
He should be back today (I predict, and/or he is obliged to do so)

Finally, note that the meanings of possibility and ability are often more naturally expressed by **dāk** following the verb, rather than by **hóyíh** 'can':

Léihdeih jáu dāk la   (or **Léihdeih hóyíh jáu la**)
(*lit.* you leave can already)
You can leave now

Tìuh yú sihk dāk la   (or **Tìuh yú hóyíh sihk la**)
(*lit.* the fish eat can already)
The fish can be eaten

Similarly, verb + particle combinations with **m̀h** (see Unit 17) are often used to express the negative counterparts meaning 'cannot' in preference to **m̀h hóyíh**:

Chín bōng m̀h dóu léih	or	**Chín m̀h hóyíh bōng léih**
(*lit.* money help not succeed you)		(*lit.* money not can help you)
Money can't help you		Money can't help you

Ngóh wán m̀h dóu kéuih	(not	***Ngóh m̀h hóyíh wán dóu**
(*lit.* I find not succeed her)		**kéuih**)
I can't find her		

There is a subtle difference between **... m̀h dóu**, meaning inability to do something, and **m̀h ... dāk**, meaning that something is not allowed or not possible due to external circumstances:

Ngóh bōng m̀h dóu léih	I can't help you (because I lack the ability)
Ngóh m̀h bōng dāk léih	I can't help you (because I'm not allowed to, I have no time, etc.)

Consequently, inability to perceive something is expressed with **... m̀h dóu**:

Ngóh gāmyaht sēung-fūng, màhn m̀h dóu yéh
I have a cold today, (so I) can't smell anything

Ngóh lám m̀h dóu baahnfaat
I can't think of a solution

See also Unit 17 on verbs of perception.

Exercise 20.1

Translate the following using a modal auxiliary:

1 I need to go home (**fāan ūkkéi**)
2 She knows how to drive (**jā chē**)
3 I'm going to apologize (**douh-hip**)
4 My friend will take you there (**daai léih heui**)
5 You can take the train (**daap fóchē heui**)
6 We should arrive on time (**jéunsìh dou**)
7 You may leave early (**jóu jáu**)
8 I will return the books (**wàahn syū**)
9 He knows how to answer the question (**daap mahntàih**)
10 She should get married (**git-fān**)
11 She's willing to reduce the price (**gáam ga**)
12 We're willing to compromise (**tóhhip**)

13 They're not willing to wait any longer (**dáng loih dī**)
14 My wife doesn't need to attend the meeting (**hōi-wúi**)
15 We don't need to worry (**dāamsām**)

Exercise 20.2

Make the following statements negative:

1 **Ngóh sīk kéuih**	I know him
2 **Ngóh sīk heui gódouh**	I know how to go there
3 **Ngóh yiu fan-gaau**	I need to sleep
4 **Kéuih yiu faahn**	She wants rice
5 **Kéuih wúih fāan ūkkéi**	She will go home
6 **Léih hóyíh làuh dāi**	You can stay behind
7 **Léih hóyíh wuhn sāam**	You may change your clothes
8 **Ngóhdeih yīnggōi yāusīk**	We should rest
9 **Kéuih yīnggōi máaih láu**	She should buy a flat
10 **Kéuih sīk tàahn kàhm**	He knows how to play the piano

Exercise 20.3

Express the following situations using a modal verb:

1 You want to date (**yeuk**) someone
2 Undertake to inform (**tūngjī**) someone on a future occasion
3 Regret that you cannot help (**bōng**) someone this time
4 You don't need anything to eat (**sihk**)
5 Someone should drive more carefully (**síusām dī**)
6 Give someone permission to give in their homework late (**chìh dī gāau gūngfo**)
7 Tell your students they should not be so rude (**gam chōulóuh**)
8 You are not willing to pay so much (**béi gam dō chín**)
9 You do not know how to get to the post office (**heui yàuh-gúk**)
10 Your friend would not agree (**tùhngyi**)

Exercise 20.4

Add a modal adverb to the sentences provided to give the meaning indicated:

Example: **Léih yiu jóu dī sānchíng** → **Léih yātdihng yiu jóu dī sānchíng** You must apply early

1	Ngóh gām-lín wúih git-fān	I may get married this year
2	Ngóh gām-lín wúih git-fān	I will definitely get married this year
3	Kéuihdeih hái ūkkéi	They must be at home
4	Kéuihdeih hái ūkkéi	They may be at home
5	Ngóh wúih sahpyih dím jīchìhn fāan dou ūkkéi	I will definitely be home before twelve
6	Ngóh yiu sahpyih dím jīchìhn fāan dou ūkkéi	I must be home before twelve
7	Fūng seun yiu tīngyaht dou ge	The letter must arrive tomorrow
8	Fūng seun haih kàhmyaht dou ge	It must have arrived yesterday
9	Go leuhtsī yiu hóu lēk	The lawyer must be (needs to be) good
10	Go leuhtsī hóu lēk	The lawyer must be good (it seems)

Exercise 20.5

Give alternatives to the following sentences using **dāk** (see Unit 17) or **m̀h dóu**:

Example: **Léih hóyíh tái** You can take a look → **Léih tái dāk**

1	Ngóh gām-máahn hóyíh pùih léih	I can keep you company tonight
2	Ngóhdeih m̀h hóyíh yahp heui	We can't go in
3	Léih yìhgā hóyíh jáu	You can leave now
4	Hohksāang m̀h hóyíh góng daaih wah	Students may not tell lies
5	Hóyíh sihk la	We can eat (now)
6	Ngóh gāmyaht m̀h hóyíh heui	I can't go today
7	Ngóh m̀h hóyíh sihk tìhmbán	I can't eat dessert
8	Ngóh m̀h hóyíh daap léih	I can't answer you
9	Jēung gēipiu m̀h hóyíh gói	The air ticket cannot be changed
10	Nīdouh m̀h hóyíh tēng Daaihluhk dihntòih	Here we cannot hear mainland radio programmes

UNIT TWENTY-ONE
Passives

Cantonese passives are signalled by a **béi** phrase similar to the English *by* phrase. The **béi** phrase (**béi** + a noun phrase indicating the agent of the action) occurs before the verb:

Dī syutgōu béi dī sailouhjái sihk-jó
(*lit.* the ice cream by the children eaten)
The ice cream was eaten by the children

Bún syū béi go hohksāang je-jó
(*lit.* the book by a student borrowed)
The book was borrowed by a student

Ngóh go jái béi sīnsāang faht-gwo
(*lit.* my son by teacher punished)
My son has been punished by the teacher

The noun phrase denoting the agent of the action is obligatory in spoken Cantonese, in contrast to English and Mandarin which allow agentless passives. When the identity of the agent is unknown or left unspecified, the word **yàhn** 'person' or **yéh** 'thing' is used generically:

Ngóh go ngàhnbāau béi yàhn tāu-jó
(*lit.* my wallet by person stolen)
My wallet was stolen

Kéuih sèhngyaht béi yàhn ngāak
(*lit.* he often by person cheated)
He often gets cheated

Ngóh yauh béi yéh ngáauh chān
(*lit.* I again by something bitten)
I've been bitten again

Note the contrast with the English translations in which the agent is not mentioned at all.

A peculiarity of Cantonese passives is that a passive verb can still take a direct object. This applies especially to those verbs introduced in Unit 16 which take two objects, such as **tāu** 'steal', **faht** 'fine' and **mahn** 'ask':

Kéuih béi yàhn tāu-jó go ngàhnbāau
She had her purse stolen

Ngóh béi yàhn faht-jó hóu dō chín
I was fined a lot of money

Ngóh m̀h séung béi yàhn mahn gam dō yéh
I don't want to be asked so much

This possibility gives rise to alternative passive forms for the same idea:

a **Ngóh go chēpàaih béi yàhn ló-jó**   My licence has been taken away
b **Ngóh béi yàhn ló-jó go chēpàaih**   I've had my licence taken away
a **Kéuih ga chē béi yàhn johng-gwo**   Her car has been dented
b **Kéuih béi yàhn johng-gwo ga chē**   She's had her car dented

The first version provides an objective statement of events, while the second focuses on the effect on the person suffering the misfortune.

Passive meaning without béi

There are a number of ways in which Cantonese effectively avoids passives, involving constructions which appear to be passive in meaning but lack the **béi** phrase:

Gāan fóng yàuh-jó la
(*lit.* the room painted)
The room has been painted

Nī gihn sāam jeuk-gwo yāt chi
(*lit.* this blouse worn once)
This blouse has been worn once

Ga gēi juhng jíng-gán
(*lit.* the machine still mending)
The machine is still being mended

These cases may be seen as instances of topicalization – making the object the topic of the sentence by placing it first, as described in the next unit. Typically the verb has an aspect marker as in the above examples, or a verbal particle indicating the result of the action (see Unit 17):

Jek gáu wán fāan la
(*lit.* the dog found back)
The dog has been found again

Yàuhhei wáan yùhn la
(*lit.* game played finish)
The game is finished

Tìuh yú jīng hóu la
(*lit.* the fish steamed complete)
The fish is done (having been steamed)

This pattern also commonly occurs with an auxiliary (see Unit 20):

Dī cháaugā yīnggōi faht ge
(*lit.* those speculators should punish)
Those speculators should be punished

Ngóh go léui sèhngyaht yiu póuh
(*lit.* my daughter always wants carrying)
My daughter always wants to be carried

Tìuh fu sái-msái gói a?
(*lit.* the trousers need to alter or not)
Do the trousers need to be altered?

In such sentences a subject could be inserted:

Tìuh fu (ngóh) sái-msái gói a?
(*lit.* the trousers (I) need to alter or not)
Do (I) need to alter the trousers?

Nī gāan ūk (ngóhdeih) yīnggōi jōngsāu
(*lit.* this house (we) should redecorate)
(We) should redecorate this house

Nī dī yùhnjāk (yàhn-yàhn) yiu gei-jyuh
(*lit.* these principles (everyone) need remember)
(Everyone) needs to remember these principles

For the most part, however, the subject remains implicit and is understood as 'one' or 'people' in general.

Exercise 21.1

Turn the following active sentences into their passive counterparts using **béi**:

1	Ga chē jó-jyuh ngóhdeih	The car is blocking us
2	Gíngchaat jūk-jó kéuihdeih	The police have caught them
3	Dī sailouhjái gáau lyuhn-jó gāan fóng	The children have made a mess of the room
4	Nī go hohksāang yèhng-jó gó go daaih jéung	The student has won that grand prize
5	Kéuih je-jó ngóh go sáudói	She has borrowed my handbag
6	Dī chē sēng chòuh séng-jó ngóh	The noise of the cars has awakened me
7	Kéuih go làahm-pàhngyáuh máaih-jó gāan ūk	Her boyfriend has bought the house
8	Kéuihdeih jíng waaih-jó go dihnlóuh	They have broken the computer
9	Ngóh yuhng-jó dī chín	I have used the money
10	Kéuihdeih sihk-jó dī jyūgwūlīk	They have eaten the chocolate
11	Kéuih dá laahn-jó jek būi	He has broken the glass
12	Ngóh tái-gwo fūng seun	I have read the letter
13	Kéuih hōi-gwo go seunsēung	He has opened the mailbox
14	Kéuih jíng-gán ga chē	He is mending the car
15	Kéuihdeih maaih-jó fūk wá	They have sold the picture

Exercise 21.2

Turn the following sentences into passive ones by either a **béi** + **yàhn** phrase or a **béi** + **yéh** phrase (note **yáuh yàhn** meaning 'somebody': see Unit 6). In some cases there may be two alternative versions:

Example: **Yáuh yàhn chéung-jó ngóh go léuih-pàhngyáuh** Someone stole my girlfriend from me → **Ngóh go léuih-pàhngyáuh béi yàhn chéung-jó** or **Ngóh béi yàhn chéung-jó go léuih-pàhngyáuh**

1	Yáuh yàhn ló-jó ngóh go sáubīu	Someone took my watch
2	Yáuh yàhn hōi-jó douh mùhn	Someone opened the door

3 **Yáuh yàhn sīk-jó láahngheigēi**	Someone turned off the air conditioning
4 **Yáuh yàhn ngāak-jó kéuih dī chín**	Someone cheated him out of his money
5 **Yáuh yàhn máaih-jó dī syū**	Someone bought the books
6 **Yáuh yéh ngáauh dóu ngóh jek sáu**	Something has bitten my hand
7 **Yáuh dī yéh fàahn dóu kéuih**	Something has troubled him
8 **Yáuh dī yéh yínghéung dóu kéuih ge sāmchìhng**	Something has affected her mood

† Exercise 21.3

Render the passive sentences below with non-passive (topicalized) alternatives, adding an aspect marker or auxiliary where appropriate:

Example: The tuition has been paid (**béi**) → **Hohkfai béi-jó la**

1 This room (**gāan fóng**) has been booked (**dehng**)
2 The house (**gāan ūk**) is being built (**héi**)
3 The film (**tou hei**) should be seen (**tái**)
4 The book (**bún syū**) has been published (**chēutbáan**)
5 The shirt (**gihn sāam**) doesn't need to be ironed (**tong**)
6 Your plan (**go gaiwaahk**) is being considered (**háauleuih**)
7 The car (**ga chē**) has been checked (**yihm**) before
8 The picture (**fūk séung**) has been taken (**yíng**) already
9 The light (**jáan dāng**) has been turned off (**sīk**)
10 The child (**go sailouhjái**) always wants to be carried (**póuh**)

UNIT TWENTY-TWO
Word order and topicalization

For the most part, word order in Cantonese may be said to follow the pattern subject – verb – object, much as in English:

Subject	Verb	Object	
Ngóh	**jūngyi**	**kéuih**	I like him/her
Ngóh sailóu	**máaih-jó**	**gāan ūk**	My brother has bought a house

It would be more accurate, however, to say that while Cantonese can be treated in this way – this order normally works – departures from it play an important role in the language. In particular, the sentence need not begin with the subject. Indeed, the object of the verb often comes first if it represents what the sentence is felt to be about:

Nī go yàhn ngóh gin-gwo
(*lit.* this person I have seen)
I've seen this person before

Póutūng-wá ngóh sīk síu-síu
(*lit.* Putonghua I know a little)
I know a little Putonghua

Fahn boují léih báai hái bīndouh a?
(*lit.* the newspaper you put where)
Where did you put the newspaper?

This pattern is known as topicalization – making something other than the subject the 'topic' of the sentence – and while also possible in English, its use is much more widespread in Cantonese. In English it is used mostly for contrasting two things, explicitly or implicitly, and this also occurs in Cantonese:

Pìhnggwó ngóh jūngyi sihk
Apples I like to eat (but not bananas)

Chín ngóh hóyíh béi léih, sìhgaan jauh m̀h hóyíh laak
Money I can give you, but not time

Deihtit ngóh chóh-gwo, dihnchē jauh meih (chóh-gwo)
(*lit.* underground I've taken, tram then not yet)
I've been on the underground, but not the tram

Bākgīng choi ngóhdeih sihk-gwo, Chìuhjāu choi jauh meih (sihk-gwo)
(*lit.* Beijing food we have eaten before, Chiu Chow food then not yet)
We've eaten Peking food but not Chiu Chow

Note some characteristic features of sentences of this kind:

(i)   the adverb **jauh** is often added after the second topic to make the contrast more explicit;
(ii)   the predicate can be omitted in the second clause;
(iii) in many cases the most natural English translation does not put the object first; this illustrates how the Cantonese syntax 'prefers' the topicalized version.

Topic without subject

Making the object the topic usually results in the word order: object – subject – verb, as in the above examples. Remembering that the subject can be omitted, however (see Unit 4), we are often left with merely object – verb:

Sāangyaht daahn-gōu sihk-jó la
(*lit.* birthday cake eaten already)
We've eaten the birthday cake

Dī hēungbān yám saai la
(*lit.* the champagne drunk all)
The champagne is all gone

Gihn sāam tong-jó meih a?
(*lit.* the shirt ironed or not yet)
Has the shirt been ironed?

Such a pattern often appears like a passive sentence, and may be so translated (see Unit 21):

Sān gēichèuhng juhng héi-gán
(*lit.* new airport still building)
They're still building the new airport
(or: The new airport is still being built)

Ga chē hái chóng douh jíng-gán
(*lit.* the car at the garage there repairing)
They're repairing the car at the garage
(or: The car is being repaired at the garage)

Hanging topics

A less familiar, but characteristically Chinese form of topicalization occurs when the topic is neither the subject nor the object of the verb, but something more loosely related to the content of the sentence. We may distinguish several types of 'hanging topics' of this kind:

(i) The topic sets a location in time or space:

Hēunggóng jeui gwai haih jōu ūk
(*lit.* Hong Kong most expensive is rent house)
In Hong Kong the biggest expense is rent

Hahtīn ngóh jūngyi yàuh-séui
(In) summer, I like swimming

Seuhnghói ngóh yáuh pàhngyáuh, Bākgīng jauh móuh
I have some friends in Shanghai, but not in Beijing

(ii) The topic sets up a whole, of which an element later in the sentence represents a part:

Gam dō geijé jeui lēk haih kéuih
(*lit.* so many reporters most smart is him)
Of all the reporters he's the brightest

Nī go daahn-gōu kéuih sihk-jó yāt bun
(*lit.* this cake he's eaten one half)
He's eaten half of this cake

Sahp go hohksāang yáuh gáu go hóyíh yahp daaihhohk
(*lit.* ten students have nine can enter university)
Nine out of ten students can enter university

(iii) The topic states a general category of which the subject or object represents a particular type:

Síusyut ngóh tái Jūngmán faai dī
(As for) novels, I read Chinese ones faster

Bējáu léih hóyíh yám Chīngdóu
(For) beer, you can drink Tsingtao

Gwóngdūng gō, ngóh jūngyi tēng Wòhng Fēi
As far as Cantonese songs are concerned, I like to listen to Faye Wong

Exercise 22.1

Change the word order to make the object the topic of the sentence:

Example: **Ngóh meih sihk-gwo yùh-chi**   I've never eaten shark's fin
→   **Yùh-chi ngóh meih sihk-gwo**

1	**Ngóh máaih-jó gó bún syū**	I bought that book
2	**Kéuih hóu jūngyi sihk syutgōu**	She likes to eat ice cream
3	**Ngóh m̀h sīk heui Wohnggok**	I don't know the way to Mongkok
4	**Ngóhdeih tái-gwo nī tou hei**	We've seen this film
5	**Kéuih sīk góng Chìuhjāuwá**	She knows how to speak Chiuchow dialect
6	**Léih tēng-gwo nī sáu gō meih a?**	Have you heard this song before?
7	**Léih yáuh-móuh sāam baak mān a?**	Have you got 300 dollars?
8	**Kéuih heui-gwo Hóiyèuhng Gūngyún**	She has been to the Ocean Park
9	**Ngóh jeui jūngyi Sīubōng ge yāmngohk**	I like Chopin's music best
10	**Ngóh hóu tùhngyi léih ge táifaat**	I quite agree with your view

Exercise 22.2

Add a clause using **jauh** to contrast with the first (for negation in the second clause, see Unit 14):

Example: **Fūng seun sé yùhn la, bún syū jauh meih** The letter's finished, the book is not

1 **A-Ann ngóh gin-gwo, A-May** _____
   Ann I've met, May I haven't
2 **Nī gihn sāam sái-jó, gó gihn** _____
   This dress has been washed, that one . . .
3 **Wohnggok hóu fōngbihn, Sāigung** _____
   Mongkok is convenient, Sai Kung . . .
4 **Nī tou hei hóu chèuhng, gó tou** _____
   This film is pretty long, that one . . .
5 **Dihnsih ngóh yahtyaht dōu tái, dihnyíng** _____
   Television I watch every day, films . . .
6 **Kéuih mùihmúi ngóh sīk, kéuih sailóu** _____
   Her sister I know, her brother . . .
7 **Oujāu ngóh heui-gwo, Méihgwok** _____
   Australia I've been to, America . . .
8 **Léih ge tàihyíh ngóh jipsauh, kéuih ge** _____
   Your suggestion I accept, his . . .
9 **Yàuh-séui ngóh hohk-gwo, móhngkàuh** _____
   Swimming I've learnt, tennis . . .
10 **Làuhhàhng yāmngohk ngóh jūngyi, gúdín yāmngohk** _____
   Pop music I like, classical music . . .

Exercise 22.3

Express your opinion or experience of the following topics, beginning the
sentence with the phrase provided:

> Example: **Hēunggóng Dóu** . . . (Hong Kong Island): **Hēunggóng Dóu**
> **ngóh m̀h sīk louh** I don't know my way around Hong Kong Island

1 **Faai chāan** (fast food) . . .
2 **Syúga** (in the summer holidays) . . .
3 **Sailouhjái** (children) . . .
4 **Gam dō yeuhng dímsām** (of all the kinds of dim sum) . . .
5 **Sáutàih dihnwá** (mobile phones) . . .
6 **Sāam tìuh tāai** (of the three ties) . . .
7 **Yahtmán** (Japanese) . . .
8 **Páauchē** (sports cars) . . .
9 **Jūnggwok yāmngohk** (Chinese music) . . .
10 **Git-fān** (marriage, getting married) . . .

UNIT TWENTY-THREE
Yes/no questions

To ask a question to which the answer is 'yes' or 'no', Cantonese in effect asks 'verb-not-verb?' This is rather like asking 'Is X the case or not?' without the 'or' being expressed:

Kéuihdeih làih-m̀h-làih a?
(*lit.* they coming (or) not coming)
Are they coming?

Léih seun-m̀h-seun a?
Do you believe it?

Léih dáng-m̀h-dáng kéuih a?
Will you wait for her?

The same pattern applies to adjectives:

Ga chē gwai-m̀h-gwai a?	Is the car expensive?
Dī hàhngléih chúhng-m̀h-chúhng a?	Is the luggage heavy?
Léih gāan fóng daaih-m̀h-daaih a?	Is your room big?

With auxiliaries (see Unit 20), the auxiliary is repeated before the verb:

Gāmyaht wúih-m̀h-wúih lohk yúh a?
(*lit.* today will (or) will not fall rain)
Will it rain today?

Léih sīk-m̀h-sīk góng Yahtmán a?
Can you speak Japanese?

Léih yiu-m̀h-yiu heui sái-sáu-gāan a?
Do you want to go the bathroom?

Applying this pattern to the verb **haih** 'to be' we have **haih-mhaih** 'is it the case', a form which is especially useful in checking information:

Léih haih-mhaih sing Tàahm ga?   Is your surname Tam?
Ngóhdeih haih-mhaih gāmyaht heui a? Is it today we are going?

Some points to notice:

(i) The particle **a** is usually added: this is felt to make the question more polite, less of an imposition on the listener (see Unit 25).
(ii) If the verb, adjective or auxiliary being questioned has more than one syllable, only the first syllable is repeated:

jūngyi	like	**Léihdeih jūng-mh-jūngyi Hēunggóng a?**
		Do you like Hong Kong?
sānchíng	apply	**Léih sān-mh-sānchíng nī fahn gūng a?**
		Will you apply for this job?
hōisām	happy	**Léih gāmyaht hōi-mh-hōisām a?**
		Are you happy today?
chūngmìhng	smart	**Kéuih chūng-mh-chūngmìhng a?**
		Is he smart?
hóyíh	can	**Ngóh hó-mh-hóyíh chóh a?**
		Can I sit down?
yīnggōi	should	**Ngóh yīng-mh-yīnggōi douhhip a?**
		Should I apologize?

Exceptional verbs

Two common verbs have special negative forms, which also need to be used in questions. Since the negative form of **yáuh** is **móuh** (Unit 6) the question form is not *__yáuh-mh-yáuh__ but **yáuh-móuh**:

Léih yáuh-móuh sailouhjái a?   Do you have children?
Ngóhdeih yáuh-móuh sìhgaan a?   Do we have time?

We also use **yáuh-móuh** to ask a question about a past event:

Léih yáuh-móuh heui máaih yéh a? Did you go shopping?
Kàhmyaht yáuh-móuh lohk yúh a?   Did it rain yesterday?

Similarly, given that the negative counterpart of **yiu** meaning 'need' is **msái** (Unit 20), the corresponding question form is **sái-msái**:

A: **Léih sái-msái tái yīsāng a?**   Do you need to see a doctor?
B: **Yiu a** (not *sái a)   Yes

A: **Ngóh sái-msái bōng-sáu a?**   Do I need to help?
B: **Msái la, mgōi**   No, thank you

Replying to questions

The standard reply to questions of this kind is to repeat the whole verb or adjective used in the question, adding the negative word **m̀h** for a negative answer:

A: **Léih jūng-m̀h-jūngyi nīdouh a?**   (*lit.* you like (or) not like here)
                                                     Do you like it here?
B: **Jūngyi a**   (*lit.* like)
                                                     Yes (not *haih, see Unit 7)
A: **Léih heui-m̀h-heui Lèuhndēun a?**   Are you going to London?
B: **M̀h heui la**   No

Questions with meih

Another important question form uses **meih** 'not yet' which when added to a statement makes a question:

Léih sihk báau meih a?   Have you eaten enough?
Ngóhdeih wáan yùhn meih a?   Have we finished playing yet?

This form is used to ask whether an action has taken place or not, with completion signalled by verbal particles like **báau** and **yùhn** above (see Unit 17) or by the aspect markers **jó** and **gwo** (Unit 18):

Kéuih git-jó-fān meih a?   Is he married?
Kéuih git-gwo-fān meih a?   Has he ever been married?
Léih gāau-jó séui meih a?   Have you paid your taxes yet?
Léih gāau-gwo séui meih a?   Have you ever paid taxes?

The standard responses pick up the relevant part of the question as follows:
Yes – repeat the verb and aspect marker, often adding the particle **la**:

A: **Léih sīk-jó dāng meih a?**   Have you turned off the lights?
B: **Sīk-jó la**   Yes

A: **Léih heui-gwo Maahn-gūk meih a?**   Have you ever been to
                                            Bangkok?
B: **Heui-gwo la**   Yes, I have

No – repeat **meih**, typically adding the particle **a** to make the negative response less abrupt:

A: **Kéuih sīng-jó-jīk meih a?**   Has she got promoted?
B: **Meih a**   No, not yet

A: **Léih si-gwo waaht-syut meih a?**   Have you ever tried skiing?
B: **Meih a**   No, I haven't

Exercise 23.1

Form yes/no questions based on the following statements:

1 **Ngóhdeih tīngyaht heui   We're going hiking tomorrow
   hàahng-sāan**
2 **Hēunggóng yìhgā hóu yiht**   It's hot in Hong Kong now
3 **Kéuih gūngsī yáuh mahntàih**   His company has problems
4 **A-John yíhgīng fāan-jó làih**   John is back (has returned) already
5 **Léih yiu làuh háidouh a**   You need to stay here
6 **Kéuihdeih būn-jó ūk**   They've moved house
7 **Taaigwok léihdeih heui-gwo**   You've been to Thailand before
8 **Gāmyaht haih gakèih lèihge**   Today is a holiday
9 **Kéuih haih gáu yuht chēutsai ge** She was born in September
10 **Léih ūkkéi hóu yúhn ge**   Your home is a long way away

Exercise 23.2

Add an auxiliary to form a question using **wúih, yīnggōi, hóyíh, yiu/msái, sīk**:

1 **Léihdeih _____ yìhmàhn a?**   Are you going to emigrate?
2 **Tīngyaht _____ fāan-gūng a?**   Do we need to go to work
                                              tomorrow?
3 **Léih _____ jā-chē a?**   Do you know how to drive?
4 **Ngóhdeih _____ chìh dī jáu a?**   Could we leave a bit later?
5 **Léih _____ bōng ngóhdeih a?**   Would you help us?
6 **Léih _____ pùih léih ūkkéi-yàhn a?**   Will you stay with your family?

7 **Kéuih _____ je chín gāau jōu a?**	Does she need to borrow money to pay her rent?
8 **Kéuihdeih _____ jóu dī git-fān lē?**	Maybe they should get married sooner?
9 **Léih _____ hingjūk sāangyaht a?**	Will you have a birthday celebration?
10 **Ngóh _____ gám yéung jouh a?**	Should I act this way?

Exercise 23.3

Answer the following questions, alternating positive and negative answers:

1 **Léih ūkkéi yáuh-móuh dihnlóuh a?**	Do you have a computer at home?
2 **Kéuih yáuh-móuh bóuhím a?**	Does he have insurance?
3 **Nī go haih-mhaih lóuhbáan a?**	Is this the boss?
4 **Haih-mhaih léih sé ge?**	Did you write this?
5 **Léihdeih wúih-m̀h-wúih git-fān a?**	Will you get married?
6 **Léih háau-jó síh meih a?**	Have you had your exams yet?
7 **Léih heui-gwo Seuhnghói meih a?**	Have you been to Shanghai?
8 **Kéuih fan-jó meih a?**	Has she gone to sleep yet?
9 **Léih gaau yùhn syū meih a?**	Have you finished teaching?
10 **Ga chē johng-gwo meih a?**	Has the car been in an accident?

UNIT TWENTY-FOUR
Wh-questions

Wh-questions involve the 'wh-words' *who, what, where,* and so on. Their Cantonese equivalents are mostly based on the interrogative forms **bīn, géi** and **dím**:

bīn ...	which?	**géi ...**	how ...?
dím (yéung)	how?	**mātyéh**	what?
bīngo	who?	**géisìh**	when?
dímgáai	why?	**jouh mātyéh**	why?
bīndouh	where?	**géi dō**	how many?

Syntax of questions

Instead of coming at the beginning of the question as in English, the Cantonese question words come wherever the corresponding word or phrase would come in a plain statement:

Statement	Question
Ngóh tàahn kàhm	*Bīngo tàahn kàhm a?*
I play the piano	Who plays the piano?
Ngóh gin dóu *Peter*	**Léih gin dóu *bīngo* a?**
(*lit.* I see Peter)	(*lit.* you see who)
I saw Peter	Who did you see?
Ngóh sihk *mihn*	**Léih sihk *mātyéh* a?**
(*lit.* I eat noodles)	(*lit.* you eat what)
I'm eating noodles	What are you eating?
Ngóh heui *Yīnggwok*	**Léih heui *bīndouh* a?**
(*lit.* I go England)	(*lit.* you go where)
I'm going to England	Where are you going?

Ngóh *tīngyaht* jáu
(*lit.* I tomorrow leave)
I'm leaving tomorrow
Nīdouh yáuh yú sihk
(*lit.* here have fish eat)
There are fish to eat here

Léih *géisìh* jáu a?
(*lit.* you when leave)
When are you leaving?
Bīndouh yáuh yú sihk a?
(*lit.* where have fish eat)
Where are there fish to eat?

Similarly, 'how' and 'why' usually come between the subject of the sentence and the verb, like the corresponding phrase in a statement:

Ngóhdeih *daap bāsí* heui
   gēichèuhng
(*lit.* we take bus go airport)
We go to the airport by bus

Ngóhdeih *dím yéung* heui
   gēichèuhng a?
(*lit.* we how go airport)
How do we get to the airport?

Ngóh *yānwaih kéuih* gam sēungsām
(*lit.* I because (of) him so sad)
I'm so sad because of him

Léih *dímgáai* gam sēungsām a?
(*lit.* you how come so sad)
Why are you so sad?

Kéuih *waih-jó ngóh* m̀h yiu fahn
   gūng
(*lit.* he on account of me not take
   the job)
He turned down the job for my sake

Kéuih *dímgáai* m̀h yiu fahn
   gūng a?
(*lit.* he how come not take the
   job)
Why did he turn down the job?

Alternatively, **dímgáai** 'why' can also begin the question:

Dímgáai léih gam sēungsām a?   Why are you so sad?
Dímgáai kéuih m̀h làih hōi mùhn gé?   Why doesn't he open the door?

Jouh mātyéh (*lit.* 'do what?') is an alternative expression for 'why' questions:

Kéuih jouh mātyéh gam lāu a?
(*lit.* she do what so angry)
Why is she so angry?

Léih jouh mātyéh kéih háidouh a?
(*lit.* you do what stand here)
What are you standing there for?

Jouh mātyéh usually asks the purpose behind someone's doing something, while **dímgáai** (*lit.* 'how to explain?') asks the reason for it.

Questions and politeness

Note that the sentence particle **a** is usually added at the end, as in other types of question (Unit 23). Without it, the question would sound abrupt and even impolite: for example, if you are asking why someone is doing something, which already represents something of an intrusion. A way to make such a question more polite is to add **Chéng mahn** 'May I ask' as well as **a**:

Chéng mahn yìhgā géi dím a?	May I ask what time it is?
Chéng mahn léih gwai sing a?	May I ask what your surname is?

This formula is especially appropriate for asking questions of strangers.

Interrogative phrases

bīn 'which' combines with the classifier appropriate to the noun concerned (see Unit 8); the noun itself can either be included or be understood:

Léih jūngyi bīn fūk (wá) a?	Which (picture) do you like?
Ngóhdeih máaih bīn tìuh (yú) a?	Which (fish) shall we buy?
Léih go léui duhk bīn gāan (hohkhaauh) a?	Which (school) does your daughter go to?

géi 'how (many)' combines with adverbs and adjectives to form question phrases such as **géi loih** 'how long' and **géi dō** 'how many/how much':

Léih làih-jó Hēunggóng géi loih a?	How long have you been in Hong Kong?
Léih tìuh fu géi chèuhng a?	How long are your trousers?
Ngóh tùhng léih góng-gwo géi dō chi a?	How many times have I told you?
Daap bāsí yiu géi dō chín a?	How much does it cost to take the bus?

Note also the phrases **géi dō seui** to ask a person's age and **géi dím (jūng)** to ask the time:

Léih go jái géi dō seui a?
(*lit.* your son how many years)
How old is your son?

Ngóhdeih géi dím chēut mùhnháu a?
(*lit.* we what time go out door)
What time do we leave?

Exercise 24.1

Form questions by substituting a question word for the phrase in bold italic type:

Example: ***Peter*** **dá dihnwá làih** → **Bīngo dá dihnwá làih a?**

1a *Ngóh pàhngyáuh* **hái heiyún dáng ngóhdeih**
    My friend is waiting for us at the cinema
b   **Ngóh pàhngyáuh** *hái heiyún* **dáng ngóhdeih**
    My friend is waiting for us *at the cinema*
2a **Kéuihdeih tīngyaht heui** *Dōlèuhndō*
    They are going *to Toronto* tomorrow
b   **Kéuihdeih** *tīngyaht* **heui Dōlèuhndō**
    They are going to Toronto *tomorrow*
3a **Gām máahn yáuh** *yú* **sihk**
    There's *fish* for dinner tonight
b   *Gām máahn* **yáuh yú sihk**
    There's fish for dinner *tonight*
4a **Ngóh daap bāsí heui** *hohkhaauh*
    I go *to school* by bus
b   **Ngóh** *daap bāsí* **heui hohkhaauh**
    I go to school *by bus*
5a **Kéuih waih-jó** *dī jáiléui* **yìhmàhn**
    She emigrated for *the children's sake*
b   **Kéuih** *waih-jó dī jáiléui* **yìhmàhn**
    She emigrated *for the children's sake*
6a **Léih jyuh-jó (hái)** *Méihgwok* **sahp lìhn la**
    You have been living *in America* for ten years
b   **Léih jyuh-jó (hái) Méihgwok** *sahp lìhn* **la**
    You have been living in America *for ten years*

Exercise 24.2

Form questions to elicit information as follows:

1 Ask what your friend is eating (**sihk**)
2 Ask a friend when he will come back (**fāan làih**)

3 Ask what time the plane (**fēigēi**) departs (**héifēi**)
4 Ask where someone lives (**jyuh**)
5 Ask why there is nobody here (**móuh yàhn**)
6 Ask a child her age (**seui**)
7 Ask why your friend is late (**chìh-dou**)
8 Ask what time the library (**tòuhsyū-gwún**) closes (**sāan mùhn**)
9 Ask where you can buy a train ticket (**fóchē fēi**)
10 Ask why the door is closed (**sāan-jó**)

Exercise 24.3

Ask for directions in a polite way by starting with **Chéng mahn** 'May I ask':

1 How to get to Kowloon Tong MTR station (**Gáulùhngtòhng deihtit jaahm**)
2 How to get to the Chek Lap Kok Airport (**Chek Lahp Gok Gēichèuhng**)
3 Where is the restroom (**sáisáugāan**)/toilet (**chisó**)?
4 How to get to the top floor (**déng láu**)?
5 How to get to the post office (**yàuh-gúk**)?
6 Where are the restaurants (**chāantēng**) in this hotel (**jáudim**)?
7 Which bus goes to the Star Ferry (**Tīnsīng Máhtàuh**)?
8 Which ferry (**syùhn**) goes to the Discovery Bay (**Yùhgíng-wāan**)?
9 Where is the nearest supermarket? (**jeui káhn ge chīukáp-síhchèuhng**)?
10 Where is the minibus station (**síubā jaahm**)?

UNIT TWENTY-FIVE
Sentence particles

Sentence particles are one of the most challenging features of Cantonese for learners of the language. Without them, many Cantonese sentences sound incomplete, abrupt, or even impolite. Cantonese has a rich repertoire of particles which serve a variety of communicative functions in different speech contexts, and are probably best learnt from direct experience. Below we introduce some of the most basic and frequently used particles, bearing in mind that there are altogether some thirty particles in use.

Perhaps the most basic particle is **a**, because of its importance for politeness and in asking questions. It is the most common, and most neutral, of the sentence particles, serving to soften the force of a statement or question.

a is regularly used in questions, as we have seen in Units 23–24:

Léih heui-m̀h-heui kéuih ūkkéi a?	Are you going to his house?
Kéuih haih-mhaih jyuh hái Sātìhn a?	Does she live in Shatin?
Ngóhdeih heui bīndouh sihk-faahn a?	Where shall we go to eat?

a can also be used in affirmative sentences, for example, to soften the force of a negative response (see Unit 24):

A: **Léih haih-mhaih msyūfuhk a?**	Are you sick?
B: **Mhaih a**	No

mē is used in a particular kind of question, expressing surprise or the unexpected:

Léih m̀h jī mē?	Don't you know?
Ngóhdeih m̀h gau mē?	Don't we have enough?

(**mē** should not be confused with the Mandarin question particle **ma**, which has no real counterpart in Cantonese.)

Another important particle is **ge**, which appears in assertions, especially together with **haih** (see Unit 7):

Kéuih jouh wuhsih ge	She's a nurse
or: **Kéuih haih jouh wuhsih ge**	
Ngóh séung bōng kéuih ge	I want to help her
or: **Ngóh haih séung bōng kéuih ge**	

jē serves to play down the extent or significance of something:

Géi baak mān jē	It's just a few hundred dollars
Hóu yùhngyih jē	It's really pretty easy
Ngóhdeih heui wáan háh jē	We're just going to have some fun

la adds a sense of current relevance to the statement. It is comparable to Mandarin **le**, although rather less widely used. It occurs especially with the perfective aspect **-jó** and other particles expressing completion such as **hóu** and **yùhn**:

Kéuihdeih lèih-jó-fān hóu loih la	They have been divorced for some time
Kéuih bún jihjyún sé hóu la	Her autobiography is written up
Ngóh tái yùhn go bougou la	I've finished (reading) the report

lā and **ā** are used primarily in imperatives and requests (see Units 26–27):

Léih síusām dī lā	Do be careful
Mgōi béi būi séui ngóh ā	(Give me) a glass of water, please

Of the two, **lā** is rather more insistent while **ā** is more neutral.

Particle combinations

The expressive range of particles is greatly increased by combinations. **ge**, for example, can be followed by almost any particle:

Gó tou dihnsih-kehk jouh yùhn *ge la*	That soap opera has finished now
Kéuih góng-siu *ge jē*	He's only joking
Léih yíhwàih ngóh sòh *ge mē?*	Do you think I'm stupid?

In this way three or more particles can readily occur together:

Léih sīk louh *ge la mē*?
Do you (really) know the way?

Kéuih haih síuhohk-sāang *lèihge je wo*!
She's only a primary school student, you know!

Normally the particles have their usual contributions, so that rather than learning how to use, say, the combination **ge la**, the learner should concentrate on individual particles and the combinations will tend to look after themselves.

Contractions: ge + a = ga

This contraction of two particles already introduced illustrates another way in which particles combine. Take a typical statement ending with **ge**:

Nī go bougou haih kéuih sé ge
(*lit.* this report is he wrote)
It was him who wrote this report

Kéuih haih sing Làhm ge
(*lit.* he is surnamed Lam)
His surname is Lam

Putting these sentences into question form, which requires the particle **a**, we end up with **ga**:

Nī go bougou haih-mhaih kéuih sé ga?	Was it him who wrote this report?
(not * **Nī go bougou haih-mhaih kéuih sé ge a?**)	
Kéuih haih-mhaih sing Làhm ga?	Is his surname Lam?
(not * **Kéuih haih-mhaih sing Làhm ge a?**)	

Similarly **lèihge**, itself a combinaton of **lèih** and **ge**, becomes **lèihga** in questions through fusion with **a**:

Nī go ngóh pàhngyáuh lèihge	This is my friend
Haih-mhaih léih pàhngyáuh lèihga?	Is he your friend?

Exercise 25.1

Add an appropriate particle at the end of each sentence (choose from **jē, lā, la, ge, ga, lèihga**):

1	**Dī mihn sihk dāk** _____	The noodles are ready to eat
2	**Dī mihn m̀h sihk dāk** _____	The noodles cannot be eaten (are inedible)
3	**Ngóh jihnghaih tái-háh** _____	I'm just looking
4	**Ngóh sailóu jouh wuihgaisī** _____	My younger brother is an accountant
5	**Làahmyán haih gám ge** _____	Men are like that
6	**Mgōi léih bōng ngóh sé** _____	Please write it for me
7	**Ngóhdeih yíhgīng fān-jó-sáu** _____	We've already split up
8	**Nī go haih tīnchòih yìhtùhng** _____	This is a child prodigy, you see
9	**Léih hōisām dī** _____	(Try to) be happier!
10	**Kéuih jāang ngóh hóu síu chín** _____	He owes me very little money

Exercise 25.2

Add an appropriate particle to complete the following questions (choose from **a, mē, ga, lèihga**):

1	**Léih giu mātyéh méng** _____?	What is your name?
2	**Nī go mātyéh** _____?	What is this?
3	**Dím wúih gam gwai** _____?	How come it's so expensive?
4	**Gāmyaht haih Sīngkèih Yaht** _____?	Is it really Sunday today?
5	**Léih yám-m̀h-yám yéh** _____?	Will you have a drink?
6	**Géidím gin gaausauh** _____?	What time do we see the professor?
7	**Léih m̀h sīk jā-chē ge** _____?	Don't you know how to drive?
8	**Haih-mhaih léih sé** _____?	Was it you who wrote it?

Exercise 25.3

Match the sentence with the translation based on the particle:

1	**Kéuih séung bōng léih ge**	a	He only wants to help you
2	**Kéuih séung bōng léih mē**	b	He wants to help you
3	**Kéuih séung bōng léih jē**	c	Does he really want to help you?
4	**Léih góng béi kéuih tēng lā**	d	Are you going to tell her?
5	**Léih wúih góng béi kéuih tēng mē**	e	Would you really tell her?

6 **Léih wúih-m̀h-wúih góng béi kéuih**   f   Why don't you tell her?
   tēng a
7 **Kéuihdeih git-jó-fān ge la mē**   g   Are they married?
8 **Kéuihdeih git-jó-fān ge la**   h   What, they're married?
9 **Kéuihdeih git-jó-fān meih a**   i   They're already married

UNIT TWENTY-SIX
Imperatives

Imperatives are a type of sentence telling someone to act, as in commands and requests. While English drops the subject pronoun in imperatives, Cantonese typically retains it:

Léih bōng-sáu lā
(*lit.* you help hand)
Help me

Léih joi góng yāt chi ā
(*lit.* you again say one time)
Repeat (that) once more

Léihdeih gān ngóh làih lā
(*lit.* you follow me come)
Come with me

Note that a particle such as **lā** or **ā** is needed to distinguish an imperative from a statement; of the two, **lā** is more insistent and **ā** more neutral. The pronoun **léih** can be dropped, especially in emergencies, but this is less usual than in English and tends to be less polite:

Dá dihnwá bougíng lā!	Call the police!
Faai dī hōi mùhn lā!	Hurry up and open the door!
Gau mehng a!	Help!

To make a request more polite, **mgōi** 'please' can be added at the beginning or end of the sentence (see Unit 27):

Mgōi léih góng daaih sēng dī ā?	Could you speak louder?
Léih làih jip ngóh ā, mgōi?	Could you come and pick me up, please?

Note the use of **bōng** (*lit.* 'help') meaning to do something for another's benefit, which is often used in imperatives:

> **Léih bōng ngóh sé lā**
> (*lit.* you help me write)
> Write it for me, will you? (not: *Help me write it)

> **Mgōi léih bōng ngóh hōi dāng ā?**
> (*lit.* please you help me open light)
> Would you turn on the light for me?

Although **bōng** on its own can mean 'help', in this construction it means that the addressee is expected to perform the action himself/herself.

Adjectives too can be used in imperatives, but call for the use of **dī** (*lit.* 'a little'):

Léih síusām dī lā!	Be careful!
Mgōi léih síngmuhk dī lā!	Please try to be smart!
Léihdeih láahngjihng dī lā!	Calm down a bit!

Compare the use of **dī** in comparatives (see Unit 12) and similarly with adverbial constructions (see Unit 10):

Léih hah chi jyú dāk hóu-sihk dī lā!	(*lit.* you next time cook good-to-eat more)
	Can you cook a bit better next time?
Léih jāp dāk jeng dī lā! (colloquial)	Try to dress better!
Mgōi léih góng dāk maahn dī lā!	Please speak a bit more slowly!
Léih faai dī jāp yéh jáu!	Hurry up and pack to leave!

Prohibitions: mhóu

Negative imperatives are marked by **mhóu** 'don't' (*lit.* 'no good') between the subject and the verb. Here the pronoun can be freely omitted:

Mhóu heui lā	Don't go
(Léih) mhóu jáu jyuh	Don't leave yet
(Léihdeih) mhóu aai-gāau lā	Don't argue

Again the pattern is applicable to adjectives too, often with **gam** 'so':

Mhóu gam bēigwūn lā!	Don't be so pessimistic!

(Léih) mhóu gam sēungsām lā!	Don't be so sad!
(Léihdeih) mhóu chòuh lā!	Don't be (so) noisy!

Similarly with adverbial constructions:

(Léih) mhóu jā dāk gam faai lā!	Don't drive so fast
(Léih) mhóu tō gam loih lā!	Don't delay too long

An alternative marker for negative imperatives is **máih**, usually used without the pronoun:

Máih chòuh lā!	Don't be (so) noisy!
(Léih) máih jáu jyuh!	Don't go yet!
Máih chēut sēng lā!	(*lit.* don't produce (a) sound)
	Shut up!

As these examples suggest, commands with **máih** tend to be more abrupt or impatient than those with **mhóu,** and used when there is a close relationship between the speaker and addressee.

First person imperatives: let's . . .

A different kind of imperative is the first person plural ('let's . . .'). Here the pronoun **ngóhdeih** ('we') may be retained or dropped:

Ngóhdeih fāan heui sīn	Let's go back
Jáu lā!	Let's go!
Yātchàih sihk lā	Let's eat together

The adverb **bātyùh** 'rather' is often added here, before or after **ngóhdeih**:

Bātyùh ngóhdeih heui wáan lā!	Why don't we go and have some fun!
Ngóhdeih bātyùh jóu dī jáu ā	Let's leave early

Negative counterparts can be formed by adding **mhóu** before the verb, just as for second-person imperatives:

Ngóhdeih mhóu gam sām-gāp lā	Let's not be so impatient
Ngóhdeih bātyùh mhóu góng kéuih lā	Let's not talk about him

Exercise 26.1

Add a particle to the following statements to form imperatives:

1	Léih sé-seun béi ngóh	Write to me
2	Léih faai dī fāan ūkkéi	Come home quickly
3	Maahn-máan hàahng	Walk slowly
4	Síusām gwo máhlouh	Cross the street carefully
5	Jīkhāak béi chín	Pay immediately
6	Yám dō dī séui	Drink more water
7	Jóu dī fong gūng	Get off work as early as you can
8	Tàuh ngóh yāt piu	Vote for me
9	Dáng ngóh yāt jahn	Wait for me a while
10	Lám chīngchó dī	Think more clearly

Exercise 26.2

Make negative counterparts of the imperatives given:

Example: **Léih sāan mùhn lā** Close the door, will you? → **Léih mhóu sāan mùhn lā**

1	Léih hōi chēung lā	Open the window, will you?
2	Léih góng lohk heui lā	Carry on speaking, will you?
3	Léih maaih-jó gāan ūk lā	Sell the house, will you?
4	Léih sihk yeuhk lā	Take the medicine, will you?
5	Léih gói tàihmuhk lā	Change the topic, will you?
6	Léihdeih gaijuhk góng lā	Do carry on talking
7	Ngóhdeih heui lā	Let's go
8	Léihdeih faai dī kyutdihng lā	Hurry up and decide
9	Léih bātyùh jyun gūng lā	Why don't you change your job?
10	Ngóhdeih bātyùh būn ūk lā	Let's move house

Exercise 26.3

Use **bōng** to make requests out of the following statements:

Example: **só mùhn** lock the door (for me) → **léih bōng ngóh só mùhn ā**

1	máaih sung	buy groceries (for me)
2	gei seun	send the mail (for me)

3 **yíng séung**   take a picture (for us)
4 **gahm jūng**   ring the bell (for him)
5 **gāau hohkfai**   pay tuition (for them)
6 **jíng chē**   fix the car (for us)
7 **jouh daahn-gōu**   make a cake (for her)
8 **jyú-faahn**   cook a meal (for us)
9 **dehng gēipiu**   book an air ticket (for me)
10 **wán gūng**   find a job (for him)

Exercise 26.4

Form imperatives with the adjectives provided:

Example: tell someone to be happy (**hōisām**): **Léih hōisām dī lā!**

1   ask a friend to be more optimistic (**lohk-gwūn**)
2   tell a guest not to be so polite (**haakhei**)
3   encourage a student to be diligent (**kàhnlihk**)
4   tell a child not to be so greedy (**tāam-sām**)
5   ask someone to be more civilized (**sīmàhn**)
6   tell someone not to be so proud (**gīu-ngouh**)
7   ask someone to speak louder (**daaih sēng**)
8   ask your friend not to walk (**hàahng**) so fast (**faai**)
9   tell a friend not to dress (**jeuk**) so casually (**chèuihbín**)
10 ask your spouse not to be so stubborn (**ngaahng-géng**)

UNIT TWENTY-SEVEN
Requests and thanks

Polite requests

Requests typically use imperative sentences as introduced in Unit 26. To make a request in a polite way, **mgōi** 'please' is used either at the beginning or at the end of the utterance. Note that the particle **ā** or **lā** is necessary so that the request does not sound abrupt (see Units 25–26):

Mgōi béi būi yiht chàh ngóh ā?	May I have a cup of hot tea, please?
Béi yāt go seunfūng ngóh ā, mgōi?	May I have an envelope, please?

Alternatively, **mgōi léih** is used with the pronoun **léih** present:

Mgōi léih béi fahn boují ngóh ā?	May I have a newspaper, please?
Hàahng faai dī lā, mgōi léih	Walk faster, will you

Invitations which are a form of request are initiated by **chéng** which means 'invite':

Chéng yahp làih chóh ā	Come in and have a seat, please
Chéng chóh dāi maahn-máan góng ā	Sit down and talk slowly, please

Compare also the polite formulation **Chéng mahn** 'May I ask' (Unit 24).

Thanks

Two different expressions mean 'thank you': **mgōi** and **dōjeh**. These cause some difficulty for the English speaker since the precise distinction between the two is not easily drawn, while **mgōi** also means 'please'. **mgōi** is used as a response to small favours such as opening the window, picking up a book from the floor, serving drinks or food:

A: **Ngóh bōng léih ló lā**   Let me carry it for you (*lit.* help
                                    you to carry it)
B: **Mgōi**   Thanks

Note here a common source of misunderstanding: while **bōng** literally
means 'help', in a sequence of verbs like the above it generally means to
do something *for* someone.

mgōi saai 'thank you very much' is stronger, with the particle **saai** 'all'
added for emphatic effect:

A: **Yám dō dī tōng ā?**   Have more soup, please?
B: **Hóu ā, mgōi saai**   Sure, thanks very much
A: **Ngóh bōng léih hōi mùhn lā**   Let me open the door for you
B: **Léih lèih dāk hóu hahp sìh,** You came at the right time. Thanks
   mgōi saai   very much

dōjeh is used to thank people for gifts and unexpected favours. Examples
include presents and invitations:

A: **Sung béi léih ge**   This is for you (giving someone a
                                    present)
B: **Dōjeh**   Thank you
A: **Gāmyaht ngóh chéng sihk-**   Lunch is on me today
   faahn
B: **Dōjeh saai!**   Thanks very much!
(alternatively B can insist on paying: **Ngóh chéng lā!** Let me pay!)

It also includes what might be considered metaphorical gifts, such as
compliments and congratulations:

A: **Gūnghéi léih wo!**   Congratulations!
B: **Dōjeh!**   Oh, thank you

Alternatively, the compliment can be played down in accordance with
traditional Chinese modesty:

A: **Léih gāmyaht jeuk dāk gam leng gé!**
   (*lit.* you today dress manner so beautiful)
   You're looking great today!
B: **Mhaih aak**
   Not really

Thanks of any kind can be replied to with **msái (mgōi/dōjeh)** or **msái
haakhei** all of which mean 'no need' (see Unit 20):

A: **Dōjeh léih béi ngóh ge jīchìh**   Thank you for your support
B: **Msái haakhei**   Not at all

Apologies

deui-mjyuh 'sorry' is a general apology, appropriate for minor inconveniences such as accidentally running into somebody, but also for major offences.

Deui-mjyuh, ngóh tàuhsīn m̀h yīnggōi faat pèihhei ge
Sorry, I shouldn't have got angry just now

deui-mjyuh literally means 'cannot face' and can take an object representing the person wronged, which may come after **deui-mjyuh** or between **deui** 'face' and **mjyuh**:

> **Ngóh gokdāk hóu deui-mjyuh ūkkéi-yàhn**
> I feel I cannot face my family (after what I've done)
> **Ngóh jānhaih deui-mjyuh kéuih**
> I really feel bad about what I've done to him
> (or **Ngóh jānhaih deui kéuih mjyuh**)

mhóuyisi (*lit.* '[I'm] embarrassed') is appropriate for matters such as misunderstandings and minor failures to meet expectations:

Mhóuyisi, seuihdouh sāk-chē, sóyíh ngóh chìh dou
I'm sorry, the tunnel was jammed, that's why I'm late

Mhóuyisi, ngóh làuh-jó fūng seun hái ūkkéi
Sorry, I left the letter at home

mgōi je-gwo is used to apologize for pushing through a crowd.

Exercise 27.1

Formulate the following requests using **mgōi**:

1 Give me a menu (**jēung chāanpáai**)
2 Speak slower (**maahn dī**)
3 Say it again (**joi ... yāt chi**)
4 Write faster (**faai dī**)
5 Don't turn on (**hōi**) the air conditioning (**láahnghei**)

6 Close (**sāan màaih**) the door (**douh mùhn**)
7 Ask the students to come
8 Call the police (**gíngchaat**)
9 Don't waste money (**sāai chín**)
10 Give me the bill (**dāan**)

Exercise 27.2

Make the following requests more polite by inserting **chéng** 'invite' at the beginning of the sentence and adding an appropriate particle:

1 **Làuh dāi háu seun**   Leave a message (as on an answering machine or voicemail)
2 **Gaijuhk góng lohk heui**   Continue talking again
3 **Dáng ngóh yāt jahn**   Wait for me a little while
4 **Tūngjī ngóhdeih jeui sān sīusīk** Inform us of the latest news
5 **Séuhng tòih líhng jéung**   Go on the stage to get the award
6 **Làuhsām tēng syū**   Listen to the lecture attentively
7 **Gān-jyuh ngóh hàahng**   Follow me
8 **Gwo làih nībihn chóh**   Come and have a seat over here
9 **Béi jēung gēipiu ngóh tái**   Show me your (air) ticket
10 **Sé dāi léih ge deihjí tùhng**   Write down your address and
    dihnwá houhmáh   telephone number

Exercise 27.3

Choose **mgōi** or **dōjeh** to thank someone for the following:

1 A friend opens the door for you
2 An acquaintance has treated you to dinner at a restaurant
3 A group of colleagues present you with a leaving present
4 A waiter hands you the menu
5 A colleague compliments you on your dress/suit
6 Someone calls you to the phone
7 Someone offers to give you a ride
8 When you're the seller having sold something to a client, customer
9 Someone you don't know has helped you with directions to your destination
10 Your boss congratulates you on your performance

Exercise 27.4

Express apologies as appropriate for the following situations:

1   You arrive very late for a formal business meeting
2   You inadvertently step on someone's toes
3   You forgot to return someone's call
4   You failed to do something very important as promised
5   You are pushing your way into the lift
6   You sincerely regret what you have done to someone
7   You're only a few minutes late. Your friends are waiting for you
8   You made a terrible mistake, causing your company to suffer a loss of profit
9   You have missed a deadline, causing some inconvenience
10   You have missed an important appointment

UNIT TWENTY-EIGHT
Numbers, dates and times

Lucky numbers

Our last unit, twenty-eight, falls appropriately enough on a lucky number: two (**yih**) sounds like 'easy' and eight (**baat**) rhymes with **faat** meaning 'make money, prosper' as in the Chinese New Year greeting **Gūnghéi faat chòih**, literally 'congratulations (and may you) prosper'. By contrast, four (**sei**) is an unlucky number as it rhymes with **séi** 'die' and is consequently subject to taboo: the Alfa Romeo 164 (**yāt luhk sei**) was perceived to be uncomfortably close to **yāt louh séi** ('one – road – die') so that it was renumbered for the Hong Kong market as the 168 (**yāt luhk baat/yāt louh faat** 'one – road – prosper').

Cardinal numbers

The number system is decimal and highly regular – so much so that it has been claimed to give the Chinese an advantage in mathematical tasks.

1 yāt	11 sahp-yāt	21 yih-sahp-yāt (yah/yeh-yāt)
2 yih	12 sahp-yih	22 yih-sahp-yih (yah/yeh-yih, etc.)
3 sāam	13 sahp-sāam	23 yih-sahp-sāam
4 sei	14 sahp-sei	24 yih-sahp-sei
5 ńgh	15 sahp-ńgh	25 yih-sahp-ńgh
6 luhk	16 sahp-luhk	26 yih-sahp-luhk
7 chāt	17 sahp-chāt	27 yih-sahp-chāt
8 baat	18 sahp-baat	28 yih-sahp-bāat
9 gáu	19 sahp-gáu	29 yih-sahp-gáu
10 sahp	20 yih-sahp	30 sāam-sahp

100 yāt baak 1,000,000 yāt baak maahn
1,000 yāt chīn 10,000,000 yāt chīn maahn
10,000 yāt maahn 100,000,000 yāt yīk (as used in the Hong Kong Stock Exchange)

Note some abbreviations:

• In combinations, **yih-sahp** (20) may become **yah-** or **yeh-**:

Kéuih jauhlèih yah seui ge la	She's almost twenty (years old)
Yah-sei síusìh yihtsin	Twenty-four hour hotline
Yeh-ńgh māan, mgōi	Twenty-five dollars, please

• In numbers from thirty onwards, the word **sahp** 'ten' is often reduced to **ah** as in **sà'ah-yāt** 'thirty-one', and so on.

Ngóh yáuh gáu'ah-baat go hohksāang
I have ninety-eight students

Kéuih sèhng sei'ah seui dōu mei git-fān
He's already forty but still not married

Numbers over a hundred precede the lower numbers as follows:

120	**yāt baak yih-sahp** (or simply: **baak yih**)
1,400	**yāt chīn sei baahk** (**chīn sei**)
15,000	**yāt maahn ńgh chīn** (**maahn ńgh**)

The difficulty comes above 10,000, **yāt maahn**. Above this figure Cantonese speakers count in terms of **maahn**, not **chīn** (1,000):

42,000	**sei maahn yih chīn**
360,000	**sāamsahp-luhk maahn**

Zero is **lìhng**. It is used in numbers with zero at the beginning or between digits:

0.8	**lìhng dím baat** (*lit.* nought point eight)
306	**sāam baak lìhng luhk** (*lit.* three hundred zero six)

Two: **yih** or **léuhng**?
There are two words meaning 'two':

• **yih** is used in counting and quoting numbers, days, etc.:

yih yuht yih houh	the second of February
daih yih chi	the second time (*lit.* number two time)
daih yih doih	the second generation

- **léuhng** is used, together with the classifier, in referring to a number of items:

léuhng go yàhn	two people
léuhng gihn sāam	two shirts

In a few instances either **yih** or **léuhng** can be used, for example, when the numbers 200, 2,000 and 20,000 are used before a noun:

yih/léuhng baak mān	two hundred dollars
yih/léuhng chīn bohng	two thousand pounds
yih/léuhng maahn yàhn	twenty thousand people

Ordinal Numbers

Ordinal numbers are formed, also in a highly regular way, by putting **daih** before the number:

daih yāt	first
daih yih	second (idiomatically also means 'another')
daih sāam saigaai	the third world
daih luhk lihnggám	the sixth sense

Dates

Dates are also based on a highly regular system:

- days of the week are numbered one to six from **sīngkèih yāt** (Monday) to **sīngkèih luhk** (Saturday) with the exception of **sīngkèih yaht** (Sunday);
- the months are numbered from **yāt yuht** (January) through to **sahpyih yuht** (December). Note the following pairs which are similar in form but very different in meaning:

sīngkèih yāt	Monday	vs.	**sīngkèih yaht**	Sunday
sāam yuht	March	vs.	**sāam go yuht**	three months
sahpyāt yuht	November	vs.	**sahpyāt go yuht**	eleven months

The order in dates is the reverse of the English, going from the general to the specific, beginning with the year and ending with the day, expressed by the number followed by **houh**. The formula is thus: **X lìhn Y yuht Z houh**:

e.g. September 3rd   **gáu yuht sāam houh**
      August 28   **baat yuht yìhsahp-baat houh**
      March 10, 1998   **yāt gáu gáu baat lìhn sāam yuht sahp houh**
      June 30, 2001   **yih lìhng lìhng yāt lìhn luhk yuht sāamsahp houh**

Times

The hours of day are expressed by **dím jūng** 'o'clock' or **dím** alone as follows:

X dím (jūng)	e.g.	**baat dím (jūng)**	eight o'clock
		sahp-yih dím (jūng)	twelve o'clock
X dím bun	e.g.	**léuhng dím bun**	half past two, 2.30
		sahp-yih dím bun	half past twelve, 12.30
X dím Y fān	e.g.	**yāt dím sahp fān**	1.10
		luhk dím seisahp-ńgh fān	6.45

To indicate points between the hours, Cantonese speakers colloquially use **jih** (5-minute intervals, or divisions of the clock face):

3.05	**sāam dím yāt go jih**	(or simply: **sāam dím yāt**)
3.10	**sāam dím léuhng go jih**	(or: **sāam dím yih**)
3.15	**sāam dím sāam go jih**	(or: **sāam dím sāam**)

For units less than ten minutes, **lìhng** 'zero' is usually inserted between **dím** and **fān** in the formula **X dím lìhng Y fān**:

| 7.04 | **chāt dím lìhng sei fān** |
| 9.08 | **gáu dím lìhng baat fān** |

Seconds are expressed by **míuh** in the form **dím Y fān Z míuh**:

| 1.03.09 | **yāt dím sāam fān gáu míuh** |
| 8.12.16 | **baat dím sahp-yih fān sahp-luhk míuh** |

To specify a.m. or p.m., the word for morning, and so on, precedes the time:

seuhngjau	morning	**seuhngjau sahp dím bun**	10.30 a.m.
hahjau	afternoon	**hahjau sei dím jūng**	4.00 p.m.
yehmáahn	evening	**yehmáahn gáu dím**	9.00 p.m.

Notice how the general term precedes the particular, as we saw in the case of dates above. This also applies to addresses, which thus follow the opposite order to English:

Hēunggóng Mōsīngléhng Douh nḡhsahp-luhk houh sāam láu B joh
Flat B, Third floor, 56 Mt Davis Road, Hong Kong

Gáulùhng Jīmsājéui Gānàhfān Douh sahpbaat houh deihhá
Ground floor, 18 Carnarvon Road, Tsimshatsui, Kowloon

Exercise 28.1

Read the following numbers in Cantonese:

1	34	6	1,200
2	79	7	12,000
3	106	8	24,302
4	234	9	43,545
5	818	10	315,000

Exercise 28.2

Read the following dates in Cantonese:

1	January 1	6	July 4, 1963
2	December 12	7	June 30, 1997
3	May 21	8	December 31, 1999
4	August 9	9	February 29, 2000
5	Friday 13	10	September 15, 2008

Exercise 28.3

Match the following times:

1	2.25	a	**saphyāt dím sahp**
2	1.10	b	**sāam dím sāam**
3	4.30	c	**gáu dīm bun**
4	5.40	d	**chāt dím yihsahp-luhk fān**
5	12.45	e	**baat dím yāt**
6	8.05	f	**yāt dím yih**
7	3.15	g	**nḡh dím baat**

8 11.50	h **léuhng dím ńgh**
9 7.26	i **sei dím bun**
10 9.30	j **sahpyih dím gáu**

Exercise 28.4

Practise giving the following information:

1 today's date (**gāmyaht ge yahtkèih**)
2 your birthday (**sāangyaht**)
3 your date of birth (**chēut sāng yahtkèih**)
4 your telephone number at home (**ūkkéi dihnwá**) and at work (**gūngsī dihnwá**)
5 your address (**deihjí**)

Exercise 28.5

Choose an auspicious registration number for your car and explain why it is a good choice for you.

KEY TO EXERCISES

Unit 1 Consonants

Exercise 1.2 Aspiration: the second of each pair begins with an aspirated consonant.

Exercise 1.3 1 **Jēung** 2 **Jiuh** 3 **Gwāan** 4 **Dīng** 5 **Sám** 6 **Jūng** 7 **Daaih Ou** 8 **Laih Jī Gok** 9 **Jēung Gwān Ou** 10 **Sāaugēiwāan** 11 **Daaih Gok Jéui** 12 **Sām Séui Bóu**

Unit 2 Vowels and diphthongs

Exercise 2.1 **gān** should sound like English 'gun', **fān** like 'fun', etc., while **gāan**, **fāan**, etc., should rhyme with 'barn' without the 'r' being sounded.

Unit 3 Tone

Exercise 3.4 1 **hauhmún** 2 **yàuhtíu** 3 **bunyé** 4 **sīuyé** 5 **Dākmán** 6 **tīnpáang** 7 **sāam jek díp** 8 **Oumún** 9 **yahp-yáu** 10 **fāyún**

Unit 4 Pronouns

Exercise 4.1 1 **Ngóh jyuh hái Gáulùhng** 2 **Hóu hōisām gin dóu léih** 3 **Ngóhdeih sīk kéuihdeih** 4 **Léih haih go hóu yīsāng** 5 **Léihdeih haih hohksāang** 6 **Kéuih hóu jūngyi yām-ngohk** 7 **Ngóh dá-jó-dihnwá béi lóuhbáan** 8 **Kéuihdeih heui-gwo Oumún** 9 **Kéuih geidāk ngóh** 10 **Kéuihdeih hóu gwa-jyuh ngóhdeih**

Exercise 4.2   1 kéuih   2 kéuih   3 kéuihdeih   4 kéuih   5 kéuihdeih
6 kéuihdeih   7 kéuih   8 kéuihdeih   9 ngóhdeih   10 léihdeih

Exercise 4.3   1 Jūngyi a/m̀h jūngyi a/Mhaih géi jūngyi a (Ngóh 'I' is
redundant)   2 (Kàhmyaht) hóu yiht a/lohk yúh a   3 Ngóh hóyíh
4 Tóuh-ngoh a/m̀h tóuh-ngoh a   5 Jáu-jó la/meih (jáu) a   6 Béi ngóh
7 Maaih-jó la/meih (maaih) a   8 Leng a/m̀h leng ge   9 Jíng hóu la/meih
(jíng hóu) a   10 Yáuh a/móuh a

Unit 5 Possession: ge

Exercise 5.1   1 léih go beih   2 kéuih ge/dī pàhngyáuh   3 kéuih deui
ngáahn   4 kéuih jēung tói   5 ngóh ge/dī seun   6 kéuih go sáudói
7 ngóh jek geuk   8 Hēunggóng ge tīnhei   9 gāmyaht ge/dī sānmán
10 tīngyaht ge heiwān

Exercise 5.2   1 Léih deui hàaih hóu leng wo   2 Léih gihn lāu géi dō
chín a?   3 Hēunggóng go gēichèuhng hóu daaih ga   4 Ngóh ga páauchē
waaih-jó   5 Ngóh dī chānchīk làih taam ngóh   6 Ngóh taaitáai dáng-gán
ngóh   7 Ngóh go jái jūngyi cheung-gō   8 Ngóh dī jáiléui duhk-gán jūng
hohk

Exercise 5.3   1 Nī jek sáubīu (haih) ngóh ge   2 Go gongkàhm (haih)
kéuih ge   3 Gó gāan ūk (haih) kéuihdeih ge   4 Nī dī syū (haih) léih
(deih) ge   5 Gó dī wá (haih) Chàhn Síujé ge   6 Nī go wái (haih)
ngóhdeih ge   7 Nī go baahn-gūng-sāt (haih) Làhm Sīnsāang ge   8 Dī
chín (haih) ngóh taaitáai ge

Unit   6 Possession and existence: yáuh

Exercise 6.1   1 Ngóh móuh yigin   2 Léih yáuh-móuh beimaht a?
3 Gāmyaht móuh sīusīk   4 Faatgwok yáuh-móuh Jūnggwokyàhn a?
5 Chēutbihn yáuh yàhn   6 Kéuih móuh behng   7 Léih yáuh-móuh
láihmaht a?   8 Bún syū móuh Jūngmàhnjih   9 Sātìhn yáuh-móuh fóchē
jaahm a?   10 Kàhmyaht yáuh taaiyèuhng

Exercise 6.2   1 Yáuh a/Móuh a   2 Yáuh a (ngóh yáuh géi go)/Móuh
a (yāt go dōu móuh)   3 Yáuh a/Móuh a   4 Yáuh a/Móuh a/Juhng meih
yáuh a   5 Yáuh gé, daahnhaih m̀h gau/Móuh māt a   6 Yáuh a (heui-
gwo)/Móuh a (meih heui-gwo)   7 Yáuh a/móuh a   8 Yáuh a (hóu yáuh
hingcheui)/Móuh a (móuh māt hingcheui)

Exercise 6.3   1 Léih yáuh-móuh chē a?   2 Léih yáuh-móuh hīngdaih jímuih a?   3 Léih yáuh-móuh sáutàih dihnwá a?   4 Léih yáuh-móuh heui gwo Bākgīng a?   5 Kéuih yáuh-móuh taam-gwo léih a?   6 Nīdouh móuh jeukjái   7 Hēunggóng yáuh hóu dō síubā   8 Yahpbihn yáuh móuh yàhn a?   9 Fosāt (yahpbihn) yáuh móuh hohksāang a?   10 Gāmyaht yáuh móuh hóu sīusīk a?

Unit 7 Being: **haih**

Exercise 7.1   1 mhaih a   2 haih a   3 mhaih a   4 haih a   5 mhaih a   6 mhaih a   7 haih a   8 haih a   9 haih a   10 mhaih a   11 haih a   12 haih a

Exercise 7.2   1 haih   2 haih   3 hái   4 hái   5 haih   6 haih   7 hái   8 haih   9 hái   10 haih

Exercise 7.3   1 Haih lóuhbáan góng béi ngóh tēng ge   2 Haih ngóh béi bún syū léih ge   3 Kéuih haih gām jiu jáu ge   4 Gihn sāam haih géisìh máaih ge   5 Go chēung haih bīngo hōi ge?   6 Ngóh haih hái nīdouh dáng léih ge   7 Haih kéuih taaitáai wán dóu ge   8 Kéuih haih hái Taaigwok johng chē ge

Unit 8 Noun Classifiers

Exercise 8.1   1 gān (catty) 2 dā (dozen) 3 fūng 4 bohng (pound) 5 dyuhn (portion, segment) 6 būi (glass)/jī (bottle) 7 deui (pair) 8 tou (set)

Exercise 8.2   1 Mgōi léuhng būi hùhng jáu   2 Mgōi yāt dihp cháau mihn   3 Mgōi sāam wún faahn   4 Mgōi (béi) dō deui faaijí   5 Mgōi béi jēun sēui   6 Mgōi béi yāt jēung/go chāanpáai ngóh   7 Mgōi léuhng go jáu-būi   8 Mgōi yāt wùh yiht séui   9 Mgōi yāt gihn daahn-gōu   10 Mgōi yāt būi gafē

Exercise 8.3   (A)   1b   2d   3e   4c   5a (B)   1b   2d   3e   4a   5c

Exercise 8.4   1c   2a   3e   4b   5d

Unit 9 Adjectives

Exercise 9.1 1 **Kéuih hóu leng** pretty/**hó-oi** lovely/**lēk** smart
2 **Kéuihdeih hóu yáih** naughty/**gwāai** nice, obedient/**chūngmìhng** clever
3 **Kéuih hóu lēk** smart/**yáuh hohkmahn** learned/**yáuh-méng** famous
4 **Kéuih hóu làhnggon** capable/**kàhnlihk** diligent/**yáuh láihmaauh** polite
5 **Ngóh hóu kàhnlihk** diligent/**yáuh seunsām** confident 6 **Kéuih hóu
lengjái** handsome/**lengléui** pretty/**gōu** tall 7 **Ga chē hóu yáuh-yìhng**
stylish/**taai gwai** too expensive 8 **hóu làahn-sihk** pretty bad/**géi hóu-sihk**
quite good 9 **Tīnhei hóu sāp** humid/**taai yiht** too hot 10 **Bún síusyut
hóu chèuhng** long/**géi hóu-tái** quite good (to read)

Exercise 9.2 1 **hóu sai** small/**daai** big/**syūfuhk** comfortable **ge haak-
tēng** 2 **hóu pèhng** cheap/**gwai** expensive/**dái-sihk** good value/**ge
chāantēng** 3 **hóu yāumahk** humorous/**hóu muhn** boring **ge syū** 4 **hóu
dākyi** cute/**hó-oi** lovely **ge gáujái/māaujái** 5 **hóu muhn** boring/**chèuhng**
long/**gámyàhn** moving **ge hei** 6 **hóu làahn/sām** difficult/**yáuh-yuhng** useful
ge gūngfo 7 **hóu yìhmjuhng** serious **ge mahntàih** 8 **hóu yāumahk**
humorous/**fuhjaakyahm** responsible **ge lóuhsī**

Exercise 9.3 1 **Ngóhdeih géi (gau saai) múhnyi** 2 **Kéuih gam (taai,
gau saai) lēk** 3 **Kéuihdeih taai (gam, gau saai) guih** 4 **Dī sailouhjái
gam (géi, gau saai) dākyi** 5 **Tou hei gam (taai, gau saai) lohngmaahn** 6
Dī tàuhfaat taai (gam, gau saai) dyún 7 **Dī gāsī gam (géi, gau saai)
pèhng** 8 **Go gaausauh gam (gau saai) yáuh-méng** 9 **Go hohksāang taai
(gam, gau saai) láahn** 10 **Dī séung gam (géi, gau saai) leng**

Exercise 9.4 1 **Nī dihp sung laaht-láat-déi** 2 **Dī tōng syūn-syūn-déi**
3 **Léih dī sāam sāp-sāp-déi** 4 **Tīnhei dung-dúng-déi** 5 **Kéuih faai
mihn yùhn-yún-déi** 6 **Kéuih deui ngáahn hùhng-húng-déi** 7 **Kéuih
go baahn-gūng-sāt lyuhn-lyún-déi** 8 **Lāp láu sūng-sūng-déi** 9 **Léih fu
ngáahn-géng mùhng-múng-déi** 10 **Léih lóuhgūng jeui-jéui-déi**

Unit 10 Adverbs of manner

Exercise 10.1 1 **Kéuihdeih màahn-máan hàahng fāan ūkkéi** 2 **Kéuih
hóu hīngfáhn gám gaaisiuh jihgéi** 3 **Kéuih hóu daaih-dáam gám mahn-
jó yāt go mahntàih** 4 **Kéuih hóu síusám gám só-jó douh mùhn** 5 **Ngóh
go jái hóu faai gám waak-jó géi fūk wá** 6 **Kéuih hóu lóuhlik gám hohk-
gán Gwóngdūng-wá** 7 **Dī hohksāang hóu làuhsām gám tēng-gán
yín-góng** 8 **Dī Hēunggóng hohksāang hóu hīngsūng gám yèhng-jó
béichoi** 9 **Yi-ngoih hóu dahtyìhn gám faatsāng-jó** 10 **Ngóh jūngyi hōi-
hōi-sām-sām gám hingjūk sāangyaht**

Exercise 10.2 1 Léih sé dāk hóu hóu 2 Ga fēigēi fēi dāk hóu dāi 3 Ngóhdeih fan dāk hóu syūfuhk 4 Kéuihdeih wáan dāk hóu hōisām 5 Kéuih tiu dāk hóu yúhn 6 Kéuih yíng-séung yíng dāk hóu leng 7 Ngóh yàuh-séui yàuh dāk hóu maahn 8 Kéuih cheung-gō cheung dāk hóu sai-sēng 9 Ngóh jyú-faahn jyú dāk hóu faai 10 Ngóh tiu-móuh tiu dāk hóu chā

Exercise 10.3 1 hóu síusām gám (carefully) 2 hóu yáuh-loihsing gám (patiently) 3 hóu syūfuk gám (comfortably) 4 jihng-jíng gám (quietly)/hóu lāu gám (angrily) 5 hóu chīngchó gám (clearly) 6 hóu faai gám (quickly) 7 hóu daaih sēng gám (loudly) 8 hóu làuhsām gám (attentively) 9 hóu hōisām gám (happily) 10 hóu sēungsām gám (sadly)

Unit 11 Adverbs of time

Exercise 11.1 (Note that the adverb can appear in more than one position.) 1 (Kàhmyaht) ngóh (kàhmyaht) hái Jīmsājéui 2 Kéuih ngāam-ngāam dou-jó gēichèuhng/(Tàuhsīn) kéuih (tàuhsīn) dou-jó gēichèuhng 3 (Yíhchìhn) Ngóh (yíhchìhn) gin-gwo kéuih 4 (Seuhngchi) kéuihdeih (seuhngchi) jung-jó tàuh-jéung 5 (Gójahnsìh) ngóhdeih (gójahnsìh) juhng sai 6 (Búnlòih) ngóh (búnlòih) jouh wuhsih ge 7 (Hah chi) ngóhdeih (hah chi) wán léih 8 Kéuih jīkhāak hóu lāu 9 (Daih yih sìh/daih sìh) ngóh (daih yih sìh/daih sìh) chéng léih sihk-faahn 10 (Yíhchìhn) ngóhdeih (yíhchìhn) hái Méihgwok jyuh-gwo

Exercise 11.2 1 Ngóh yāt go láihbaai dá yāt chi móhngkàuh (once a week) 2 Ngóh yaht-yaht heui yàuh-séui (everyday) 3 Ngóh máahn-máahn tái dihnsih (every night) 4 Ngóh jīu-jīu tái boují (every morning) 5 Ngóh yāt go láihbaai sái sāam chi tàuh (three times a week) 6 Ngóh yāt go yuht jín yāt chi tàuhfaat (once a month) 7 Ngóh yāt go láihbaai máaih yāt chi sung (once every week) 8 Ngóh yāt lìhn heui géi chi yāmngohk-wúi (a few times a year) 9 Ngóh yāt go yuht sihk yāt chi syutgōu (once a month) 10 Ngóh yāt go láihbaai taam yāt chi chānchīk (once a week)

Exercise 11.3 1 (Ngóh yaht-yaht) dá bun go jūngtàuh gēi 2 lihn yāt go jūngtàuh Gwóngdūng-wá 3 góng sāamsahp fānjūng dihnwá 4 jyú go bun jūngtàuh faahn 5 tēng sèhng máahn yām-ngohk 6 tái sèhng yaht syū 7 kīng yāt jahn gái 8 séuhng géi go jūngtàuh móhng 9 chūng sahp fānjūng lèuhng 10 sé yāt go jūngtàuh yahtgei

Exercise 11.4 1 géi go jūngtàuh (a few hours) 2 sèhng máahn (a whole evening) 3 yāt go hah-jau (one afternoon) 4 sèhng yaht (a

whole day) 5 **yāt go láihbaai** (one week) 6 **géi yaht** (a few days)
7 **sèhng jīu** (a whole morning) 8 **géi máahn** (a few evenings) 9 **sèhng
go yuht** (a whole month) 10 **géi lìhn** (a few years)

Unit 12 Comparison

Exercise 12.1 1 **Dī: Gāmyaht lyúhn dī** 2 **Dī: Kéuih yìhgā hōisām dī**
3 **Gwo: Ngóh go pàhngyáuh daaih gwo ngóh** 4 **Gwo: Kéuih gōu gwo
yìhchìhn hóu dō** 5 **Dī: Gām chi maahn dī** 6 **Gwo: Nī gāan
chāantēng/jáulàuh pèhng gwo gó gāan** 7 **Gwo: Ngóh jūngyi tiu-móuh dō
gwo cheung-gō** 8 **Dī: Léih ge lámfaat hóu dī**

Exercise 12.2 1 **Gāmyaht dung** (cold) **gwo kàhmyaht** 2 **Léuihjái
gwāai** (well-behaved) **gwo làahmjái** 3 **Sēutsāam gwai** (expensive)
gwo léhngtāai 4 **Dōlèuhndō (juhng) dung** (cold) **gwo Lèuhndēun**
5 **Jūngmán làahn** (difficult) **gwo Yīngmán** 6 **Yàuh-séui syūfuhk**
(comfortable) **gwo páauh-bouh** 7 **Gwóngdūng choi chēutméng** (famous)
gwo Chìuhjāu choi 8 **Jouh sāangyi sānfú** (hard) **gwo gaau-syū**

Exercise 12.3 1 **Gām-lín dung gwo gauh-lín** *hóu dō* 2 **Gāmyaht lyúhn**
hóu dō 3 **Léih dī tàuhfaat yìhgā dyún** *síu-síu* 4 **Hēunggóng gwai gwo
nīdouh** *géi púih* 5 **Ngóh** *juhng* **guih gwo kéuih** 6 **Sihk faahn** *juhng*
pèhng gwo sihk mihn 7 **Gām chi hohkfai béi seuhng chi gwai yāt baak
mān** 8 **Kéuih gōu (gwo) ngóh sāam chyun**

Exercise 12.4 A 1 **Hói-yú gwai gwo yéuhng-yú** 2 **Hēungpín hēung
gwo hùhng chàh** 3 **Làahnfā leng gwo gūkfā** 4 **Go léui daaih (gwo)
go jái léuhng seui** 5 **Nī bāan hohksāang kàhnlihk gwo gó bāan**
B 1 **Gauh hàaih béi sān hàaih syūfuhk** 2 **Yìhgā heui Oujāu béi yìhchìhn
yùhngyih(-jó)** 3 **Gūngsī gām-lín béi gauh-lín jaahn dāk dō(-jó)** 4 **Nī
bún síusyut béi daih yāt bún hóu-tái** 5 **Léih gām chi béi seuhng chi jouh
dāk hóu(-jó)**

Unit 13 Prepositions

Exercise 13.1 1 **Hohksāang hái fóng yahpbihn/douh** 2 **Jek māau hái
tói seuhngbihn** 3 **Go jámtàuh hái chòhng seuhngbihn/douh** 4 **Jī bāt hái
háp yahpbihn** 5 **Bún syū hái dang hahbihn** 6 **Go jūng hái chèuhng
seuhngbihn** 7 **Bá jē hái mùhn hauhbihn** 8 **Dī séung hái séungbóu yahp-
bihn/douh** 9 **Pō syuh hái gāan ūk chìhnbihn** 10 **Dihnsihgēi hái
syūgwaih jākbīn**

Exercise 13.2   1 chèuhng hauhbihn 2 syūgwaih seuhngbihn   3 ngàhn-hòhng deuimihn   4 máhlouh jūnggāan   5 gūngyún tùhng yàuh jaahm jīgāan 6 (chóh) hái léih jākbīn 7 háp yahpbihn/léuihmihn 8 bāanfóng chēutbihn 9 geng chìhnmihn 10 tói hahmihn 11 heung nī go fōngheung/ heung nībihn   12 yàuh jīu dou máahn

Exercise 13.3   1 Tói seuhngmihn yáuh yāt daahp syū (a pile of books) 2 Chèuhng seuhngmihn yáuh fūk wá (a picture)   3 Chyùhfóng yahpbihn móuh yàhn (nobody)   4 Haak-tēng léuihmihn yáuh géi go haakyàhn (several guests)   5 Yīgwaih yahpbihn yáuh hóu dō leng sāam (lots of nice clothes)   6 Chòhng hahmihn yáuh jek māau (a cat)   7 Dang hahbihn yáuh jī bāt (a pen/pencil)   8 Syūgwaih seuhngmihn yáuh go gūngjái (a doll)   9 Sáisáu-gāan yahpbihn yáuh tiuh mòuhgān (a towel)   10 Syūfóng yahpbihn yáuh bouh dihnlóuh (a computer)

Exercise 13.4   1 yàuh nīdouh heui yīyún   2 yàuh tòuh-syū-gwún heui faahn-tòhng 3 yàuh deih-há heui baat láu 4 heung Gáulùhng   5 gīng Tòihbāk heui Dūnggīng 6 yàuh Hēunggóng gīng Maahn-gūk heui Lèuhndēun 7 yàuh syūfóng heui chyùhfóng   8 yàuh daih yāt chi dou yìhgā 9 yàuh gēichèuhng heui ūkkéi   10 yàuh tàuh dou méih

Unit 14 Negation

Exercise 14.1   1 Kéuih ūkkéi móuh mahntàih   2 Ngóhdeih mhaih hóu guih 3 Ngóh móuh sīng-jīk   4 Kéuih gihn sāam mhaih hóu gwai   5 Ngóh tàuhsīn móuh sihk yeuhk   6 Yīsāng móuh heui douh-ga 7 Lóuhbáan mhaih hóu làu 8 Dī hohksāang móuh séuhng-móhng 9 Dī hohksāang mhaih hóu kàhnlihk   10 Gó tou hei mhaih taai chèuhng

Exercise 14.2   1 Sihk hóisīn hóu gwai (ga)   2 Wòhng Sāang chéng kéuih (a)   3 Ngóh (yáuh) duhk-gwo Faatmán (a)   4 Kéuihdeih git-jó-fān (la)   5 Ngóh bou-jó-méng (la) or Ngóh yáuh bou-méng (a)   6 Dī háausíh tàihmuhk hóu làahn (a)   7 Gāan fóng géi/hóu gōnjehng (a) 8 Kéuih yìhgā dākhàaan (a)   9 Gāmyaht yáuh tòhng   10 Ngóhdeih sihk-gwo sèh-gāng (a)

Exercise 14.3   1 **msānsīn** not fresh, stale 2 **msíusām** careless 3 **mhóuchói** unfortunate 4 **mgōuhing** discontented 5 **mgihnhōng** unhealthy 6 **mjūngyi** dislike 7 **m-mìhngbaahk** fail to understand 8 **mtùhngyi** disagree 9 **m-yānséung** not appreciate 10 **mlàuhsām** inattentive

Exercise 14.4   A 1 Kéuih mhaih móuh seunsām   2 Kéuih góng ge yéh mhaih móuh douhléih   3 Léih gājē mhaih m̀h wúih bōng léih 4 Ngóhdeih   mhaih   m̀h   gau   chín 5 Léih   gāmyaht   mhaih mdākhàahn   **B** 1 Ngóhdeih mhaih mtùhngyi 2 Ngóhdeih m̀h hóyíh m̀h jáu   3 Gūngsī mhaih m̀h háng gā yàhn-gūng   4 Ngóh m̀h wúih mgeidāk   5 Léih mhaih máaih m̀h héi

Unit 15 Verbs of motion

Exercise 15.1 1 séuhng làih ngóh ūkkéi 2 fāan heui hohkhaauh 3 séuhng heui làuhseuhng 4 gwo làih Yīnggwok 5 lohk heui séjih-làuh 6 gwo làih tái-háh 7 fāan làih taam ngóhdeih 8 yahp heui hōi-wúi 9 lohk làih sihk-faahn 10 chēut heui jouh-yéh

Exercise 15.2 1 Ngóh tīngyaht heui hohkhaauh (to school) 2 Léih làih nīdouh (here) sihk-faahn 3 Ngóh gwo heui góbihn (there) wán yàhn 4 Léih dākhàahn séuhng làih ngóh ūkkéi (my place) chóh 5 Ngóhdeih yiu fēi fāan heui Oujāu (to Australia) 6 Go léuihjái jáu chēut heui chēutbihn (outside) 7 Ngóh dī chānchīk fāan làih Hēunggóng (to Hongkong) douh-ga   8 Léih hóyíh lohk heui gwóng-chèuhng (to the shopping centre) máaih yéh 9 Ngóh jīkhāak yahp heui sái-sáu-gāan (bathroom) wuhn sāam   10 Ngóh tùhngsih gwo làih ngóh gāan fóng (to my room) kīng-gái

Exercise 15.3 1 gwo heui 2 yahp làih 3 lohk làih 4 séuhng heui 5 chēut heui 6 fāan làih 7 lohk làih/heui 8 séuhng heui 9 yahp heui/làih   10 fāan heui/làih

Exercise 15.4 1 Ga fochē fāan-jó làih 2 Dī seun gei-jó heui Méihgwok 3 Dī gúpiu sīng-jó séuhng heui gōu wái 4 Kéuih hái fóng hàahng-gán chēut làih 5 Kéuihdeih pàh-gán séuhng làih sāandéng 6 Bún syū dit-jó lohk (heui) deihhá 7 Go kàhm būn-jó gwo heui deui-mihn   8 Ga chē hōi-gán yahp làih tìhng-chē-chèuhng 9 Kéuih hàahng-gán chēut heui gāai douh   10 Kéuihdeih būn-gán lohk heui yih láu

Unit 16 Verbs of giving

Exercise 16.1 1 Béi chín ngóh taaitáai (my wife) 2 Wàahn syū béi tùhnghohk (a classmate) 3 Sung láihmaht béi léui-pàhngyáuh (one's girlfriend) 4 Gei seun béi Léih haauhjéung (Principal Li) 5 Dá-dihnwá béi gíngchaat (the police) 6 Gāau gūngfo béi sīnsāang (teacher) 7 Làuh sung béi ngóh (me) sihk 8 Máaih sāam béi go léui (daughter) jeuk   9 **Gáan tou hei béi léih** (you) **tái**   10 **Dím gō béi ngóh pàhngyáuh** (my friend) **tēng**

Exercise 16.2   1 **Kéuih sung-jó dī hēungséui béi ngóh**   2 **Yīsāng béi-jó dī yeuhk ngóh** (sihk)   3 **Ngóh wúih wàahn** (fāan) **dī màhn-gín béi léih/Ngóh wúih béi fāan dī màhn-gín léih**   4 **Lóuhbáan gyūn-jó hóu dō chín béi gaauwúi**   5 **Kéuih gei-jó fūng seun béi kéuih ūkkéi-yàhn**   6 **Ngóh je-jó jī yùhnbāt béi kéuih**   7 **Mgói béi-mín kéuih**   8 **Léih yiu wàahn** (fāan) **tìuh sósìh béi ngóh/Léih yiu béi fāan tìuh sósìh ngóh**   9 **Kéuih séung je ngóh léuhng bún syū/Kéuih séung tùhng ngóh je léuhng bún syū**   10 **Go góngsī béi-jó dī gūngfo ngóhdeih jouh**

Exercise 16.3   1 **Ngóhdeih juhng yiu béi chín kéuih** (to him)   2 **Ngóh gājē je-jó ngóh hóu dō sāam/je-jó hóu dō sāam béi ngóh** (to me)   3 **Gó go yàhn sèhngyaht tāu gūngsī** (the company) **yéh**   4 **Yáuh yàhn chéung-jó kéuih lóuhbáan** (his boss) **hóu dō chín**   5 **Ngóh heui je go tùhnghohk** (a classmate) **géi bún syū**   6 **Kéuih séung mahn sīnsāang** (the teacher) **géi yeuhng yéh**   7 **Ngóh go pàhngyáuh gaau sailouhjái** (children) **Yīngmán ge**   8 **Jingfú wúih faht gūngsī** (the company) **chín ge**

Unit 17 Verbs and Particles

Exercise 17.1   1 **dóu**   2 **dāi**   3 **fāan**   4 **gwo**   5 **dóu**   6 **yùhn**   7 **cho**   8 **hōi**   9 **dóu**   10 **dou**

Exercise 17.2   1 **Kéuih sèhngyaht tēng gújái**   2 **Ngóh tēng dóu yìuhyìhn**   3 **Kéuih yíhgīng lám dóu go daahp-on**   4 **Ngóh gin dóu go gwónggou**   5 **Léih gámgok dóu ngaatlihk**   6 **Ngóh màhn dóu yīnmeih**   7 **Kéuih jūngyi tái síusyut**   8 **Kéuih m̀h jūngyi tái hei**

Exercise 17.3   1 **Ngóh sāu m̀h dóu kéuih fūng seun**   2 **Ngóh máaih m̀h dóu hei fēi**   3 **Ngóh tái m̀h dóu/gin m̀h dóu go páai**   4 **Ngóh màhn m̀h dóu dī sung**   5 **Ngóh tēng m̀h dóu fēigēi sēng**   6 **Ngóh lám m̀h dóu dím daap**   7 **Ngóh gei m̀h dóu gam dō méng**   8 **Ngóh sihk m̀h dóu gam dō syutgōu**   9 **Ngóh wán m̀h dóu fūng seun**   10 **Ngóh pàhngyáuh heui m̀h dóu Sātìhn**

Exercise 17.4   1 **béi dāk dóu**   2 **gáau dāk dihm**   3 **tái dāk dóu**   4 **jouh dāk sèhng**   5 **seun dāk gwo**   6 **máaih dāk héi**   7 **jouh dāk chit**   8 **tēng dāk mìhng**

Unit 18 Actions and events

Exercise 18.1   1 gin-gwo   2 sái-jó   3 sihk-jó   4 tēng-gwo   5 heui-gwo
6 bou-jó-méng   7 yèhng-jó   8 háau-gwo   9 máaih-gwo   10 maaih-jó

Exercise 18.2   1 lám-gwo   2 fan-jó   3 si-gwo   4 yeuk-jó   5 sānchíng-
jó   6 johng-gwo   7 chēutbáan-jó   8 cheung-gwo   9 tái-jó   10 fāan-jó

Exercise 18.3   1 Dī hohksāang meih jáu   2 Ngóh go jái meih heui-gwo
Yīnggwok   3 Kéuih meih ló chēpàaih   4 Ngóhdeih meih jouh-gwo
jingfú gūng   5 Ngóh móuh dehng fóng   6 Go beisyū móuh fong ga
7 Ngóh meih yám-gwo Chīngdóu bējáu   8 Ngóh móuh tùhng kéuih paak-
gwo-tō   9 Dihnfai móuh gā ga   10 Lóuhbáan móuh laauh-gwo kéuih

Exercise 18.4   1f   Kéuih   chùhnglòih   meih   si-gwo   chìh   dou
2d Ngóhdeih yíhchìhn heui-gwo léih ūkkéi   3a/b Ngóh sīnsāang
yíhgīng/ngāam-ngāam   fāan-jó   séjihlàuh   4b/e   Kéuih   ngāam-
ngāam/jeuigahn sāang-jó go jái   5c/d/e Ngóh chàhnggīng/yíhchìhn/
jeuigahn háauleuih-gwo chìhjīk   6a/b Gāan jáulàuh yíhgīng/ngāam-
ngāam sāan-jó mùhn

Unit 19 Activities: **gán** *and* **jyuh**

Exercise 19.1   1 Ngóh yìhgā wuhn-gán sāam   2 Kéuihdeih kàhm-
máahn háidouh dá màhjéuk   3 Kéuih góng-gán dihnwá   4 Yìhgā
lohk-gán yúh   5 Dī sailouhjái háidouh wáan séui   6 Ngóhdeih hàahng-
gán làih   7 Kéuih yìhgā chūng-gán-lèuhng   8 Ngóh go jái háidouh
waahk-wá   9 Lóuhbáan hōi-gán-wúi   10 Kéuih juhng lāu-gán ngóhdeih

Exercise 19.2   1 Ngóh jā-jyuh tiuh sósìh   2 Kéuih máaih-gán sung
3 Ngóhdeih hóu gwa-jyuh léih   4 Léih jyú-gán mātyéh a?   5 Kéuih
yām-gán gafē   6 Dímgáai léih mohng-jyuh ngóh a?   7 Dī sailoujái
chūng-gán-lèuhng   8 Hóu dō yàhn wán-gán gūng   9 Ngóh yìhgā daap-
gán mahntàih   10 Kéuih sèhngyaht jeuk-jyuh dī gauh sāam

Exercise 19.3   1 Kéuih jeuk-jyuh sāam yàuh-séui He swims with his
clothes on   2 Kéuih līng-jyuh dī hàhngléih jáu He left carrying the baggage   3 Kéuih tái-jyuh dihnsih jouh gūngfo She does her homework while
watching television   4 Dímgáai léih m̀h mohng-jyuh ngóh góng? Why
don't you look at me while talking? 5 Ngóh jūngyi tēng-jyuh yāmngohk
yāusīk I like to relax while listening to music   6 Kéuih sèhngyaht chī-jyuh
léih go léuih heui gāai He always goes around with your daughter   7 Go
mámìh póuh-jyuh go jái chēut gāai The mother goes out carrying her son

8 **Dímgáai léih daai-jyuh ngáahn-géng fan-gaau a?** Why do you sleep with your glasses on? 9 **Ngóh lóuhgūng jā-jyuh ga sān chē làih jip ngóh** My husband is driving his new car to meet me 10 **Ngóh m̀h wúih jó-jyuh léih faat daaht** I won't get in the way of your making money

Unit 20 Auxiliary verbs

Exercise 20.1 1 **Ngóh yiu fāan ūkkéi** 2 **Kéuih sīk jā-chē** 3 **Ngóh wúih douh-hip** 4 **Ngóh pàhngyáuh wúih daai léih heui** 5 **Léih hóyíh daap fóchē heui** 6 **Ngóhdeih yīnggōi jéunsìh dou** 7 **Léih hóyíh jóu jáu** 8 **Ngóh wúih wàahn syū** 9 **Kéuih sīk daap mahntàih** 10 **Kéuih yīnggōi gịt-fān** 11 **Kéuih háng gáam ga** 12 **Ngóhdeih háng tóhhip** 13 **Kéuihdeih m̀h háng dáng loih dī** 14 **Ngóh taaitáai msái hōi-wúi** 15 **Ngóhdeih msái dāamsām**

Exercise 20.2 1 **Ngóh m̀h sīk kéuih** 2 **Ngóh m̀h sīk heui gódouh** 3 **Ngóh msái fan-gaau** 4 **Kéuih m̀h yiu faahn** 5 **Kéuih m̀h wúih fāan ūkkéi** 6 **Léih m̀h hóyíh làuh dāi** 7 **Léih m̀h hóyíh wuhn sāam** 8 **Ngóhdeih m̀h yīnggōi yāusīk** 9 **Kéuih m̀h yīnggōi máaih láu** 10 **Kéuih m̀h sīk tàahn kàhm**

Exercise 20.3 1 **Ngóh séung yeuk kéuih (chēut gāai)** 2 **Ngóh wúih tūngjī léih (ge la)** 3 **Deuimjyuh, gám chi ngóh m̀h hóyíh bōng léih/ngóh bōng m̀h dóu léih** 4 **Ngóh msái sihk yéh** 5 **Léih yīnggōi síusām dī jā-chē** 6 **Léih hóyíh chìh dī gāau gūngfo** 7 **Léideih m̀h yīnggōi gam chōulóuh** 8 **Ngóh m̀h háng béi gam dō chín** 9 **Ngóh m̀h sīk heui yàuh-gúk** 10 **Ngóh pàhngyáuh m̀h wúih tùhngyi**

Exercise 20.4 1 **Ngóh gām-lín waahkjé wúih gịt-fān** 2 **Ngóh gām-lín hángdihng wúih gịt-fān** 3 **Kéuihdeih yātdihng hái ūkkéi** 4 **Kéuihdeih hólàhng hái ūkkéi** 5 **Ngóh yātdihng wúih sahpyih dím jīchìhn fāan dou ūkkéi** 6 **Ngóh yātdihng yiu sahpyih dím jīchìhn fāan dou ūkkéi** 7 **Fūng seun yātdihng yiu tīngyaht dou ge** 8 **Fūng seun yātdihng haih kàhmyaht dou ge** 9 **Go leuhtsī yātdihng yiu hóu lēk** 10 **Go leuhtsī yātdihng hóu lēk**

Exercise 20.5 1 **Ngóh gām-máahn pùih dāk léih** 2 **Ngóhdeih m̀h yahp dāk heui/Ngóhdeih yahp m̀h dóu heui** 3 **Léih yìhgā jáu dāk** 4 **Hohksāang m̀h góng dāk daaih wah** 5 **Sihk dāk la** 6 **Ngóh gāmyaht heui m̀h dóu/Ngóh gāmyaht m̀h heui dāk** 7 **Ngóh m̀h sihk dāk tìhmbán/Ngóh sihk m̀h dóu tìhmbán** 8 **Ngóh m̀h daap dāk léih/Ngóh daap m̀h dóu léih** 9 **Jēung gēipiu m̀h gói dāk/Jēung gēipiu gói m̀h dóu** 10 **Nīdouh m̀h tēng dāk Daaihluhk dihntòih/Nīdouh tēng m̀h dóu Daaihluhk dihntòih**

Unit 21 Passives

Exercise 21.1   1 Ngóhdeih béi ga chē jó-jyuh   2 Kéuihdeih béi gíngchaat jūk-jó   3 Gāan fóng béi dī sailouhjái gáau lyuhn-jó   4 Gó go daaih jéung béi nī go hohksāang yèhng-jó   5 Ngóh go sáudói béi kéuih je-jó   6 Ngóh béi dī chē sēng chòuh séng-jó   7 Gāan ūk béi kéuih go làahm-pàhngyáuh máaih-jó   8 Go dihnlóuh béi kéuihdeih jíng waaih-jó   9 Dī chín béi ngóh yuhng-jó   10 Dī jyūgwūlīk béi kéuihdeih sihk-jó   11 Jek būi béi kéuih dá laahn-jó   12 Fūng seun béi ngóh tái-gwo   13 Go seunsēung béi kéuih hōi-gwo   14 Ga chē béi kéuih jíng-gán   15 Fūk wá béi kéuihdeih maaih-jó

Exercise 21.2   1 Ngóh go sáubīu béi yàhn ló-jó/Ngóh béi yàhn ló-jó go sáubīu   2 Douh mùhn béi yàhn hōi-jó   3 Láahngheigēi béi yàhn sīk-jó   4 Kéuih dī chín béi yàhn ngāak-jó/Kéuih béi yàhn ngāak-jó dī chín   5 Dī syū béi yàhn máaih-jó   6 Ngóh jek sáu béi yéh ngáauh dóu/Ngóh béi yéh ngáauh dóu jek sáu   7 Kéuih béi dī yéh fàahn dóu   8 Kéuih ge sāmchìhng béi dī yéh yínghéung dóu/Kéuih béi dī yéh yínghéung dóu sāmchìhng

Exercise 21.3   1 Nī gāan fóng dehng-jó (la)   2 Gāan ūk (juhng) héi-gán   3 Tou hei yīnggōi tái   4 Bún syū chēutbáan-jó (la)   5 Gihn sāam msái tong (la)   6 Léih go gaiwaahk (juhng) háauleuih-gán   7 Ga chē yihm-gwo (la)   8 Fūk séung yíng-jó (la)   9 Jáan dāng sīk-jó (la)   10 Go sailouhjái sèhngyaht yiu póuh

Unit 22 Word order and topicalization

Exercise 22.1   1 Gó bún syū ngóh máaih-jó   2 Syutgōu kéuih hóu jūngyi sihk   3 Wohnggok ngóh m̀h sīk heui   4 Nī tou hei ngóhdeih tái-gwo   5 Chìuhjāuwá kéuih sīk góng   6 Nī sáu gō léih tēng-gwo meih a?   7 Sāam baak mān léih yáuh-móuh a?   8 Hóiyèuhng Gūngyún kéuih heui-gwo   9 Sīubōng ge yām-ngohk ngóh jeui jūngyi   10 Léih ge táifaat ngóh hóu tùhngyi

Exercise 22.2   1 A-May jauh meih   2 gó gihn jauh meih   3 Sāigung jauh móuh gam fōngbihn   4 gó tou hóu dyún   5 dihnyíng jauh hóu síu tái   6 kéuih sailóu ngóh jauh m̀h sīk   7 Méihgwok jauh juhng meih   8 kéuih ge ngóh jauh m̀h jipsauh   9 móhngkàuh ngóh jauh meih hohk-gwo   10 gúdín yāmngohk ngóh jauh móuh gam jūngyi

Exercise 22.3   1 Faai chāan ngóh m̀h séung sèhngyaht sihk (I don't want to eat it that often)   2 Syúga ngóhdeih heui-jó léuihhàhng (We went on holiday)   3 **Sailouhjái sāang léuhng go jauh gau la** (To have two is enough)   4 **Gam dō yeuhng dímsām móuh yāt yeuhng hóu-sihk** (Not one dish was good)   5 **Sáutàih dihnwá gachìhn yuht làih yuht pèhng** (The prices get cheaper and cheaper)   6 **Sāam tìuh tāai jeui leng nī tìuh** (This one looks best)   7 **Yahtmán ngóh géi séung hohk** (I'd quite like to learn it)   8 **Páauchē ngóh máaih m̀h héi** (I can't afford one)   9 **Jūnggwok yāmngohk ngóh m̀h suhk** (I'm not familiar with it)   10 **Git-fān jeui gányiu mhóu gam jóu** (The most important thing is not to do it too soon)

Unit 23   Yes/no questions

Exercise 23.1   1 **Ngóhdeih tìngyaht heui-m̀h-heui hàahng-sāan a?** 2 **Hēunggóng yìhgā yiht-m̀h-yiht a?**   3 **Kéuih gūngsī yáuh-móuh mahn-tàih a?**   4 **A-John fāan-jó làih meih a?**   5 **Léih sái-msái làuh háidouh a?**   6 **Kéuihdeih būn-jó ūk meih a?**   7 **Taaigwok léihdeih heui-gwo meih a?**   8 **Gāmyaht haih-mhaih gakèih lèihga?**   9 **Kéuih haih-mhaih gáu yuht chēutsai ga?**   10 **Léih ūkkéi yúhn-m̀h-yúhn a?**

Exercise 23.2   1 **Léihdeih wúih-m̀h-wúih yìhmàhn a?**   2 **Tìngyaht sái-m̀h-sái fāan-gūng a?**   3 **Léih sīk-m̀h-sīk jā-chē a?**   4 **Ngóhdeih hó-m̀h-hóyíh chìh dī jáu a?**   5 **Léih wúih-m̀h-wúih bōng ngóhdeih a?** 6 **Léih wúih-m̀h-wúih pùih léih ūkkéi-yàhn a?**   7 **Kéuih sái-m̀h-sái je chín gāau jōu a?**   8 **Kéuihdeih yīng-m̀h-yīnggōi jóu dī git-fān lē?**   9 **Léih wúih-m̀h-wúih hingjūk sāangyaht a?**   10 **Ngóh yīng-m̀h-yīnggōi gám yéung jouh a?**

Exercise 23.3   1 **yáuh a/móuh a**   2 **yáuh a/móuh a**   3 **haih a/mhaih a**   4 **Haih a/mhaih a**   5 **wúih a/m̀h wúih a**   6 **háau-jó la/meih a**   7 **heui-gwo la/meih a**   8 **fan-jó la/meih a**   9 **gaau yùhn la/meih a**   10 **johng-gwo la/meih a**

Unit 24   Wh-questions

Exercise 24.1   1a *Bīngo* **hái heiyún dáng ngóhdeih a?**   1b **Ngóh pàhngyáuh** *hái bīndouh* **dáng ngóhdeih a?**   2a **Kéuihdeih tìngyaht heui** *bīndouh* **a?**   2b **Kéuihdeih** *géisìh* **heui Dōlèuhndō a?**   3a **Gām máahn yáuh** *mātyéh* **sihk a?**   3b *Géisìh* **yáuh yú sihk a?**   4a **Ngóh daap bāsí heui** *bīndouh* **a?**   4b **Ngóh** *dímyéung* **heui hohkhaauh a?**   5a **Kéuih waih-jó** *bīngo* **yìhmàhn a?**   5b **Kéuih** *dímgáai* **yìhmàhn a?**   6a **Léih jyuh-jó (hái)** *bīndouh* **sahp lìhn a?**   6b **Léih jyuh-jó (hái) Méihgwok** *géi loih* **a?**

Exercise 24.2   1 Léih sihk-gán mātyéh a?   2 Léih géisìh fāan làih a?
3 Fēigēi géi dím héifēi a?   4 Léih jyuh hái bīndouh a?   5 Dímgáai móuh
yàhn háidouh a?   6 Léih géi dō seui a?   7 Dímgáai léih chìh dou a?/Léih
dímgáai chìhdou a?   8 Tòuhsyū-gwún géi dím sāan mùhn a?   9 Bīndouh
hóyíh máaih fóchē fēi a?   10 Dímgáai douh mùhn sāan-jó a/gé?

Exercise 24.3   1 Chéng mahn dím heui Gáulùhngtòhng deihtit jaahm
a?   2 Chéng mahn dím heui Chek Lahp Gok Gēichèuhng a?   3 Chéng
mahn sáisáugāan/chisó hái bīndouh a?   4 Chéng mahn dím heui déng láu
a?   5 Chéng mahn dím heui yàuhjinggúk a?   6 Chéng mahn nī gāan
jáudim ge chāantēng hái bīndouh a?   7 Chéng mahn bīn ga bāsí heui
Tīnsīng Máhtàuh a?   8 Chéng mahn bīn ga syùhn heui Yùhgíng-wāan
a?   9 Chéng mahn jeui káhn ge chīukāp-síhchèuhng hái bīndouh a?
10 Chéng mahn síubā jaahm hái bīndouh a?

Unit 25 Sentence Particles

Exercise 25.1   1 la (ge la)   2 ga (ge)   3 jē   4 ge   5 la   6 lā   7 la
(ge la)   8 lèihga   9 lā   10 jē

Exercise 25.2   1 a   2 lèihga   3 ga   4 mē   5 a   6 a   7 mē   8 ga
(ge)

Exercise 25.3   1b   2c   3a   4f   5e   6d   7h   8i   9g

Unit 26 Imperatives

Exercise 26.1   1 Léih sé-seun béi ngóh lā (ā)   2 Léih faai dī fāan ūkkéi
lā (ā)   3 Maahn-máan hàahng (lā) ā   4 Síusām gwo máhlouh lā
5 Jīkhāak béi chín lā   6 Yám dō dī séui lā   7 Jóu dī fong gūng lā (ā)
8 Tàuh ngóh yāt piu lā (ā)   9 Dáng ngóh yāt jahn ā (lā)   10 Lám
chīngchó dī lā (ā)

Exercise 26.2   1 (Léih) mhóu hōi chēung lā or Máih hōi chēung
lā   2 Léih mhóu góng lohk heui lā   3 (Léih) mhóu maaih(-jó) gāan ūk
lā   4 (Léih) mhóu sihk yeuhk lā   5 (Léih) mhóu gói tàihmuhk lā
6 Léihdeih mhóu gaijuhk góng lā   7 Ngóhdeih mhóu heui lā   8 Léihdeih
mhóu gam faai kyutdihng lā   9 Léih bātyùh mhóu jyun gūng lā
10 Ngóhdeih bātyùh mhóu būn ūk lā

Exercise 26.3   1 Léih bōng ngóh máaih sung ā (lā)   2 Léih bōng ngóh
gei seun ā (lā)   3 Mgōi léih bōng ngóhdeih yíng séung ā   4 Léih bōng

kéuih gahm jūng lā (ā)   5 Léih bōng kéuihdeih gāau hohkfai lā (ā)
6 Léih bōng ngóhdeih jíng chē ā   7 Léih bōng kéuih jouh daahn-gōu ā
(lā)   8 Léih bōng ngóhdeih jyú-faahn lā (ā)   9 Léih bōng ngóh dehng
gēipiu ā (lā)   10 Léih bōng kéuih wán gūng lā (ā)

Exercise 26.4   1 Léih lohk-gwūn dī lā   2 Mhóu gam haakhei lā!
3 Léih kàhnlihk dī lā!   4 Léih mhóu gam tāam-sām lā   5 Mgōi léih
sīmàhn dī lā!   6 Léih mhóu gam gīu-ngouh   7 Mgōi léih góng (dāk)
daaih sēng dī lā   8 Mhóu hàahng (dāk) gam faai lā!   9 Mhóu jeuk dāk
gam chèuihbín lā   10 Léih mhóu gam ngaahng-géng lā!

Unit 27 Requests and thanks

Exercise 27.1   1 Mgōi béi jēung chāanpáai ngóh ā/Béi jēung chāanpáai
ngóh ā, mgōi   2 Mgōi góng maahn dī ā   3 Mgōi joi góng yāt chi ā
4 Mgōi sé faai dī ā   5 Mgōi léih mhóu hōi láahnghei ā   6 Sāan màaih
douh mùhn ā, mgōi   7 Giu dī hohksāang lèih ā, mgōi   8 Giu gíngchaat
ā, mgōi   9 Mgōi léih mhóu sāai chín lā   10 Mgōi béi jēung dāan ngóh
ā/Màaih dāan ā, mgōi

Exercise 27.2   1 Chéng (léih) làuh dāi háu seun ā/lā   2 Chéng (léih)
gaijuhk góng lohk heui ā/lā   3 Chéng (léih) dáng ngóh yāt jahn ā/lā
4 Chéng (léih) tūngjī ngóhdeih jeui sān sīusīk ā/lā   5 Chéng (léih) séuhng
tòih líhng jéung ā/lā   6 Chéng (léih) làuhsām tēng syū lā   7 Chéng (léih)
gān-jyuh ngōh hàahng ā/lā   8 Chéng (léihdeih) gwo làih nībihn chóh
ā/lā   9 Chéng (léih) béi jēung gēipiu ngóh tái ā   10 Chéng (léih) sé dāi
léih ge deihjí tùhng dihnwá houhmáh ā/lā

Exercise 27.3   1 mgōi   2 dōjeh   3 dōjeh   4 mgōi   5 dōjeh   6 mgōi
7 mgōi   8 dōjeh   9 mgōi   10 dōjeh

Exercise 27.4   (deui-mjyuh is always acceptable)   1 deui-mjyuh
2 mhóuyisi 3 mhóuyisi 4 deui-mjyuh 5 mhóuyisi/mgōi je-gwo 6 deui-
mjyuh   7 mhóuyisi   8 deui-mjyuh   9 mhóuyisi   10 deui-mjyuh

Unit 28 Numbers, dates and times

Exercise 28.1   1 sāamsahp-sei   2 chātsahp-gáu   3 yātbaak-lìhng-
luhk   4 yihbaak-sāamsahp-sei   5 baat baak yātsahp-baat   6 yātchīn
yihbaak (chīn-yih)   7 yāt maahn-yihchīn (maahn-yih)   8 yih maahn sei
chīn sāam baak lìhng-yih   9 sei maahn sāam chīn ńgh baak seisahp-
ńgh   10 sāamsahp-yāt maahn ńgh chīn

Exercise 28.2 1 yāt yuht yāt houh 2 sahpyih yuht sahpyih houh
3 ńgh yuht yihsahp-yāt houh 4 baat yuht gáu houh 5 sahpsāam houh
sīngkèih ńgh 6 yāt gáu luhk sāam lìhn chāt yuht sei houh 7 yāt gáu
gáu chāt lìhn luhk yuht sāamsahp houh 8 yāt gáu gáu gáu lìhn sahpyih
yuht sāamsahp-yāt houh 9 yihlìhnglìhnglìhng lìhn yih yuht yihsahp-gáu
houh 10 yih lìhng lìhng baat lìhn gáu yuht sahpńgh houh

Exercise 28.3 1h 2f 3i 4g 5j 6e 7b 8a 9d 10c

Exercise 28.4 1 Gāmyaht haih yātgáugáugáu lìhn sahp yuht sahp
houh 2 Ngóh ge sāangyaht haih sahp yuht sāamsahp-yāt houh 3 Ngóh
ge chēutsāng yahtkèih haih yāt gáu luhk yih lìhn gáu yuht sāam houh
4 Ngóh ūkkéi dihnwá haih yih luhk lìhng gáu chāt lìhng yāt gáu/Ngóh
gūngsī dihnwá haih yih baat ńgh gáu yih chāt yih yih 5 Ngóh ge deihjí
haih Gáulùhng Sìhng Lyùhnhahp Douh yāt baak houh sāam láu C joh

GLOSSARY OF GRAMMATICAL
TERMS

adjective   a class of words used to describe nouns.

adverb   a class of words used to describe verbs or to modify sentences.

antonym   a word having the opposite meaning to another, e.g. *unclear* as opposed to *clear*.

aspect   a grammatical distinction involving whether an event is seen as complete (as in the Cantonese perfective form **-jó**) or ongoing, as in the English progressive form *-ing* and Cantonese **-gán**.

auxiliary   a class of words used together with a verb and carrying a grammatical function, e.g. **wúih** (will).

classifier   a class of words used to 'classify' nouns by shared features such as shape or function, e.g. **tìuh** for elongated objects as in **tìuh yú** (fish).

demonstrative   words indicating proximity (this) or distance (that).

digraph   a combination of letters representing a single sound, e.g. **ng, eu**.

diphthong   a combination of two vowel sounds, e.g. **au** as in **sau** (thin).

experiential   a form of the verb denoting experience, or something which has happened at least once (expressed by **gwo** in Cantonese).

hanging topic   an instance of topicalization in which the topic is not subject or object of the verb, but bears a loose relation to the subject or object.

localizer   a class of words used after a noun to specify location, e.g. **yahp-bihn** (inside).

measure   similar to classifier; more precisely, those classifiers which denote a measured quantity, e.g. **yāt dā gāidáan** 'a dozen eggs'.

minimal pair   a pair of words or sentences differing in only one feature.

modal   having to do with possibility and necessity, as opposed to fact.

modality   the field of meaning involving possibility and necessity.

negation   forms used to deny the truth of a statement.

particle   a word which does not belong to any of the major word classes but plays a grammatical or communicative role. **Verb particles**, such as **dóu** indicating completion of an action, appear after the verb, while

sentence particles, like **a** added to questions for politeness, come at the end of the sentence.

passive   a type of sentence which shows action being done to the subject.

perfective   a form of the verb denoting an event viewed as complete (expressed by the suffix **-jó** in Cantonese).

predicate   the part of the sentence which says something about the subject, typically a verb or adjective.

preposition   a word which precedes a noun (more precisely a noun phrase), indicating a spatial or other relationship to it.

pronoun   a word which substitutes for a noun (more precisely a noun phrase, i.e. the noun and any modifiers which go with it).

topicalization   the process by which some constituent is placed first in the sentence, so that the sentence appears to be 'about' that constituent, e.g. **ga chē ngóh juhng meih maaih** (The car I haven't sold yet).

transitive verb   a verb that can or must take a noun as its object, e.g. **hit**.

INDEX

Printed in the United States
70929LV00006B/125

9 780415 193856